Charles Dowding

Compost

Charles
Dowding
Compost

Transform waste into new life

Contents

MY COMPOST STORY

The old saying goes that "the answer lies in the soil," but after 40 years of market gardening, I would add, "and the compost heap"! Experience has taught me that when it comes to improving soil to produce healthy growth, it is compost that provides the answers we need.

Soil fertility means far more than just feeds to supply the nutrients essential for plant growth; a thriving ecosystem of life within soil is what really builds enduring abundance. Compost feeds the existing web of underground life, as well as adding more microbes. These busy soil organisms—and the structure they help establish within the soil—enable roots to find the food, moisture, and air they need. The result is vigorous and healthy plants.

Compost first caught my attention as a young man, when I noticed that my mother's messy-looking heap transformed her weeds and waste into something quite different—sweet-smelling and soft-textured compost. Intrigued, I did some reading and discovered that compost had been big news during the 1940s. Soil Association journals from that time contain fascinating compost articles by the organic market gardener J. Arthur Bowers, botanist and mycologist Dr. M. C. Rayner, and soil chemist Sir Albert Howard, plus many farmers and gardeners.

Rayner and Howard ran trials where small additions of compost produced increases in growth that were far greater than could be explained by the nutrients the compost contained. This led them to study soil microbial life, and inspired Howard

to research soil biology and the amazing role of fungi in soil. Rayner uncovered the work of German scientist A. B. Frank, who in 1885 had been the first to publish evidence of mycorrhizal fungi interacting with plant roots.

Yet by the 1980s, when I started out, this knowledge of soil biology was largely forgotten or ignored. I remember being very disappointed that the thinking in horticulture at that time was that the mycelial network of fungi was not used by vegetable plants for their growth, because that did not feel right to me. Commercial growing was still in a postwar drive to maximize productivity, based on nutrients supplied by chemical (synthetic) fertilizers. This devalued compost and animal manures, which by volume are comparatively low in nutrients. The same thinking dominated horticulture, with gardeners working to feed their plants instead of their soil without realizing that applications of synthetic fertilizers reduce microbial activity and therefore soil fertility (see pp.25 26).

Since that time, I have practiced and developed my no dig gardening methods, where a 1in (2.5cm) layer of unsifted compost is spread once a year on the surface of undisturbed soil. I have found that this simple approach enables phenomenal growth right through the year while making it easy to control weeds. The amazing results in my garden at Homeacres, in Somerset, have inspired The Royal Horticultural Society, Royal Botanic Gardens, Kew, and many others to adopt a no dig approach. Compost is being rediscovered.

Creating your own compost heap allows you to convert waste plant materials into this valuable living resource with the power to transform your garden, and it's easier than you might imagine. In this book, I use understandings I've gained from decades of compost making to strip away the myths and misconceptions surrounding composting, and leave you empowered with a sound knowledge of how the process works. Without unnecessary work and complication, it's surprising how little time and energy is needed to produce a high-quality product that's easy to use and isn't full of weed seeds.

Above all, I want this book to spark your own interest in composting and bring you success so you can improve the health of your soil, your plants, yourself, and the wider environment.

" Creating your own compost heap allows you to convert waste plant materials into this valuable living resource with the power to transform your garden, and it's easier than you might imagine. "

Chapter 1

Why gardens need compost

WHAT IS COMPOST?

There is nothing complicated about compost, but it's a word sometimes used incorrectly to describe other materials with a similar appearance. A clear understanding of basic terms helps avoid confusion.

Compost

Compost is made up of organic matter (carbon-based materials derived from plants or animals) at a stage of decomposition that can vary. The term compost simply refers to any organic matter—like leaves, roots, garden prunings, and vegetable peelings—that has decomposed or broken down to the point that most of those original materials are not recognizable. Compost has a dark brown color and ideally, but not always, a soft and crumbly texture. It is not a stable product, but it will continue to decompose, reducing in volume as it does so. What comes from a compost heap is never perfectly even or finished, but it is always a valuable resource for your garden.

Soil

Clay, sand, silt, and other minerals combine with organic matter to form the soil in which gardens, farmed crops, and forests grow. Soil rarely contains more than 10 percent organic matter: 3 to 5 percent is enough to benefit soil health, while 5 to 10 percent is desirable for growing great vegetables.

Manure

Animal dung, with or without bedding materials, is called manure. Animals from which manure is gathered eat plant material, so their fresh manure is digested organic matter that will decompose to become compost after about a year, just like garden or kitchen waste. Composted manure from horses, chickens, and other farm animals is ideal for garden use. Gardeners use the term manure to differentiate the origin of this compost, as they would use leaf mold to describe compost made solely from fallen leaves (see p.124).

WHAT ABOUT "HUMUS"?

Humus is a confusing term that is used to describe stable forms of organic matter within soil. Compost is not humus. Humus could be described as the next stage, resulting from the further decomposition of organic matter, possibly over a very long time. Stable organic matter does exist within soils, but scientists have only been able to isolate it by subjecting soil to highly alkaline (pH13) solutions. This has prompted doubts that the substance known to science and studied as "humus" exists in soil under normal conditions.

WHY USE COMPOST?

Compost on the soil surface is a quick and simple way to create healthy, nourished, well-drained soil. When nurtured in this way, soil has a soft surface for sowing, has a wonderful structure for root growth, and is able to provide plants with nutrients without any need for additional feeds or fertilizers.

Compost mulches imitate nature

A mulch is anything spread or lying on the surface of soil. Adding compost as a mulch nourishes soil in the same way as the natural accumulation and decomposition of fallen leaves and other organic material on the soil surface of pastures and woodland. A compost mulch on the soil surface is just adding this organic matter in a form that is already at least partially decomposed.

The microbes responsible for decomposition convert the constituents of composted materials into complex organic compounds. This process continues as compost is further broken down after it is spread, providing a reliable source of food for other bacteria and fungi in the soil, which play key roles in helping plants obtain the nutrients and moisture needed for growth (see pp.22–24).

Practical with quick results

The joy of compost is that it's easy to use at any time of year and quickly effective. I spread compost on my no dig beds in fall mostly to feed soil organisms and protect soil from winter rain. Compost's complex organic compounds contain water-insoluble nutrients, which are not leached by rainfall, unlike those found in most fertilizers (see p.26). When spread as a mulch, it's possible to sow and plant into compost immediately, covering weedy ground so that it can quickly be converted into productive beds.

Compost is a good growing medium in itself. It is ideal for sowing seeds and has the nutrients and open structure that suit small plants while they establish before they root down into the soil. This makes it much better than undecomposed mulches, such as hay or straw. Plus it does not harbor slugs, which is a major drawback of undecomposed mulches in damp climates.

COMPOST MULCHES IMITATE NATURE

A compost mulch forms a layer of organic material on the soil surface, similar to a natural accumulation of decaying plant material. This makes it the ideal way for gardeners to feed soil life, which in turn provides the nutrients plants need for strong, healthy growth.

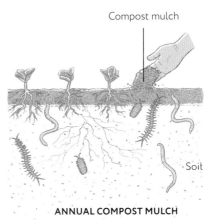

Decomposing organic matter

Fallen leaves

Compost mulch

Soil

Soil

NATURAL LEAF LITTER

ANNUAL COMPOST MULCH

THE BENEFITS OF
HOMEMADE COMPOST

Like anything else in the garden, a compost heap takes time, effort, and materials to manage successfully. I firmly believe that the benefits it will bring both you and your garden will make this investment worthwhile.

Recycling garden waste

Gardens are constantly generating what are often called waste materials, but all those grass clippings and prunings are actually a valuable resource. Turning this material into something useful is incredibly empowering. Recycling your own waste into compost that will improve your soil not only gives you a sense of how this cycle of life fits together, but also saves money that might have been spent disposing of waste and buying compost in. It comes with many environmental benefits, too, including reduced emissions from transporting waste and compost, less waste going to landfills, and a reduction in plastic packaging from purchased compost.

Brimming with beneficial microbes

Don't worry if finished compost looks a bit lumpy, because it will still be packed with invisible bacteria and fungi that boost soil's microbial life and help make nutrients more available to plants (see pp.22–24). The unique value of homemade compost is that it contains microbes native to your garden that are well adapted to survive in your climate and soil. These multiply during decomposition, so that you're adding lots of them to your soil

every time you mulch. In contrast, many commercial composts (see pp.34–35) are produced rapidly at high temperatures, which kills most of these microbes.

Good for gardeners, too

Composting can have significant benefits for our own health and well-being. With the key insights I explain here, making compost is straightforward, and you need not worry about creating a perfectly uniform end product. The satisfaction and sense of achievement that comes with spreading your own compost on soil and seeing plants flourish is just so positive. You can observe the process unfold and see wildlife make a home in your heap, all of which brings you closer to nature. Research also suggests that exposure to bacteria found in soil and compost (*Mycobacterium vaccae*) can reduce inflammation, counter feelings of stress, and activate brain neurons to produce the "happy hormone" serotonin.

66 The satisfaction and sense of achievement that comes with spreading your own compost on soil and seeing plants flourish is just so positive. **99**

NOURISHING THE SOIL COMMUNITY

Feeding soil does not mean pumping it full of nutrients. Instead, it's about using compost to build up and sustain the extraordinary array of life that can be found within healthy soil. The interactions of these creatures with each other, and directly with plants, improve conditions for root growth and actively supply plants with water and nutrients.

The soil food web

A kaleidoscope of life exists largely unseen within the soil. Each organism—from microscopic bacteria and fungi, to worms and centipedes, to mammals such as moles—feeds on living or dead plant and animal matter, decomposing it through digestion into excretions of organic compounds. These enrich soil and provide food for other creatures and plants. This complex network of interactions forms what biologists call the "soil food web."

Compost mulches work with nature

Nature's process is for soil life to feed on plant and animal material as it falls onto the soil surface, helping it decompose. The beauty of spreading compost on top of soil is that it duplicates this natural process, as well as speeding it up, because decomposition is already underway. Applying compost in this way, without incorporating it into soil, means no disturbance to soil structure (see pp.27–28) and life. It also keeps compost open to the air, which is important for keeping the organisms within it alive and working.

In gardens, compost and no dig methods can quickly improve interactions between plant roots and soil, facilitating access to the food and moisture needed for growth. The decomposed organic matter in compost provides easily accessible food for the soil food web, and compost microbes increase the population of bacteria and fungi in the soil. These microbes have the ability to unlock latent nutrients in soil that are sometimes inaccessible to plant roots without their help (see pp.22–24). An annual compost mulch maintains soil in a biologically fertile state, enabling healthy and strong plant growth without any further additions to the soil.

❝ In gardens, compost and no dig methods can quickly improve interactions between plant roots and soil, facilitating access to the food and moisture needed for growth. ❞

HOW PLANTS OBTAIN NUTRIENTS

Plant roots can absorb water-soluble nutrients directly from soil, but these easily accessible forms aren't always available in the quantities needed for healthy growth. Increasingly, scientific research is revealing the extent to which plant roots rely on relationships with soil bacteria and fungi to access the nutrients they require.

Microbial interactions with roots

Many people are aware that plants from the Legume family, such as peas, form root nodules that provide a home for *Rhizobium* bacteria that can fix nitrogen from the atmosphere. Recent research suggests that many, and possibly even all, other plants are also able to extract a range of nutrients from soil microbes that enter the growing tips of their roots, in a process dubbed "rhizophagy" (see right). This discovery shows the importance of soil microorganisms and their intrinsic role in plant growth.

Microbes are attracted to growing root tips by energy-rich "exudates" that roots produce, which contain carbohydrates that are a product of photosynthesis. Once microbes have gathered nearby, root hairs can envelop and feed from them. Their nutrient-rich cell walls are stripped by reactive oxygen released by the plant. Some microbes are killed during this process, while others are "cloned" and multiply within the root. Their presence stimulates the formation of fine root hairs, from which they are released back into the soil, where they feed on more carbon-rich root exudates and soil nutrients before the process is repeated.

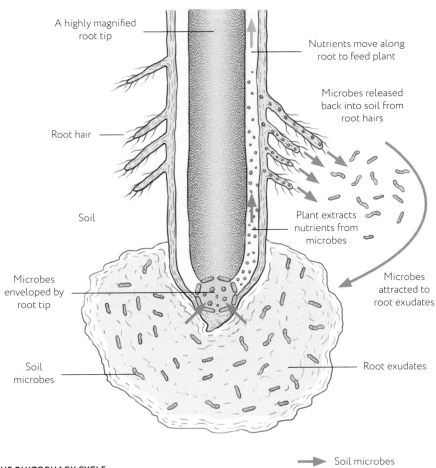

A highly magnified root tip

Nutrients move along root to feed plant

Microbes released back into soil from root hairs

Root hair

Soil

Plant extracts nutrients from microbes

Microbes enveloped by root tip

Microbes attracted to root exudates

Soil microbes

Root exudates

Soil microbes

Nutrients

THE RHIZOPHAGY CYCLE

Many types of plants harvest nutrients from soil microbes by releasing energy-rich exudates from root tips. Microbes feeding on these exudates are absorbed into roots, where their outer cell wall is broken down to supply nutrients to the plant. Surviving microbes are released back into soil to repeat the cycle.

The mycorrhizal network

More than 90 percent of plants have also forged mutually beneficial relationships with species of "mycorrhizal" fungi, which form extensive networks of very fine rootlike filaments in soil, known as mycelia. These filaments create physical links with plant roots and are able to furnish plants with a far greater supply of nutrients and moisture than they could obtain alone. They do this in exchange for energy-rich carbohydrates and lipids manufactured by the plant during photosynthesis, which nourish the fungus. This relationship is valuable to many plants and essential for some, because fungal mycelium extends far beyond a plant's root zone; can reach water and nutrients in tiny soil pores inaccessible to plant roots; and can extract valuable nutrients, such as phosphorous, from soil where plants cannot. Compost promotes a healthy soil environment where mycorrhizal fungi can thrive, and no dig leaves the mycelial network undisturbed.

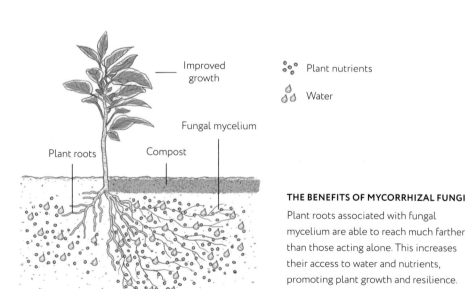

Improved growth

Plant nutrients

Water

Fungal mycelium

Plant roots

Compost

THE BENEFITS OF MYCORRHIZAL FUNGI

Plant roots associated with fungal mycelium are able to reach much farther than those acting alone. This increases their access to water and nutrients, promoting plant growth and resilience.

COMPOST vs. CHEMICAL FEEDS

Ensuring that plants are well fed is much more than simply inundating their roots with nutrients. As we've seen, it's a complex biological process, which compost enables in a much more proactive and healthy way than synthetic fertilizers.

Compost is not fertilizer

A fertilizer is any natural or manufactured substance that is added to soil to supply plant nutrients, including nitrogen (N), phosphorous (P), and potassium (K). Although compost contains lower concentrations of nutrients than a fertilizer, it enables plants to access nutrients that in most cases are already there by boosting microbial life in the soil. The beauty of this for the gardener is its simplicity, because compost makes a consistent supply of nutrients available to plants so they can access what they need when they need it. Facilitating these natural processes removes the guesswork involved in fertilizer use, where you have to try and supply the nutrients a plant needs at a particular time.

Fertilizers also damage soil microbial life, because when large doses of easily accessible nutrients are delivered around plant roots, they have no need to produce exudates to feed soil microbes (see pp.22–23). This reduces the activity of soil bacteria and fungi and makes gardeners increasingly reliant on fertilizers to support plant growth. Research on wheat crops has shown that applying inorganic fertilizer reduces both the species richness and diversity of bacteria around roots, leaving plants with far fewer beneficial bacteria to help promote their growth.

Prevention of nutrient loss through leaching

Fertilizers supply nutrients in water-soluble forms so roots can take them up quickly. This means, however, that they are easily washed (leached) from the soil by rain or irrigation, beyond the reach of roots and causing pollution in water courses. Nutrients in compost come in more complex, water-insoluble forms that need to be unlocked by microbial activity before they can be taken up by plants. These are less likely to leach from the soil and can be accessed by roots when required. I add 1in (2.5cm) of compost to no dig beds each November, before the winter rains, and continue to see luxuriant growth right through to the following fall. This couldn't happen if nutrients were leaching from the soil.

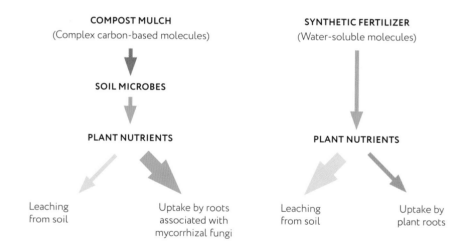

COMPOST MULCH
(Complex carbon-based molecules)

SOIL MICROBES

PLANT NUTRIENTS

Leaching from soil

Uptake by roots associated with mycorrhizal fungi

SYNTHETIC FERTILIZER
(Water-soluble molecules)

PLANT NUTRIENTS

Leaching from soil

Uptake by plant roots

NUTRIENT RETENTION IN SOIL

Compost's nutrients remain in the soil and are released gradually as microbes break down the organic material, whereas fertilizers give a quick boost of nutrients before being washed away.

BUILDING SOIL STRUCTURE

The addition of compost to soil, combined with no dig methods, promotes the work of soil organisms that create a healthy and stable soil structure. This has many benefits, including holding more life and air in soil, improving drainage, and providing firm anchorage for roots.

A glue called glomalin

The benefits of encouraging the growth of mycorrhizal fungi in soil may go beyond aiding roots in search of food and moisture. In 1996, a scientist named Sarah Wright discovered a persistent protein that could make up as much as 30 percent of the organic matter in soil. This protein was named "glomalin" and is produced in the cell walls of mycorrhizal fungi, possibly to strengthen filaments and allow them to transport water. When these mycelial filaments die, they deposit this gluelike substance in soil, where it can contribute to the formation of "aggregates" made up of soil particles and organic matter.

A stable structure benefits plants

The fact that glomalin is tough and not water soluble allows aggregates to persist in undisturbed soil, creating a stable crumb structure that retains nutrients and is beneficial to soil life, plants, and gardeners. Spaces, known as pores, are left between the unevenly sized aggregates in soil, creating room for air and water both to remain within soil and to move through it. These tiny gaps also provide space for root growth and possibly for microbes and other soil life to find a home.

Any kind of soil cultivation breaks up aggregates and interferes with the complex structure of soil. Traditionally, gardeners have been taught that soil needs to be loosened for plants to root into it, but that's not the case. Digging damages soil life, including mycorrhizal networks; makes soil more prone to erosion; and does not benefit drainage.

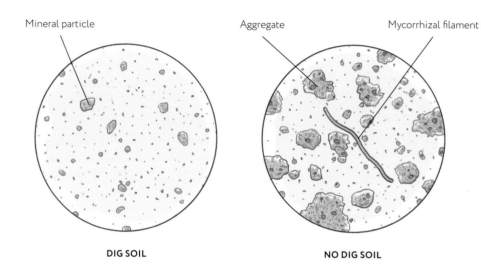

Mineral particle   Aggregate   Mycorrhizal filament

DIG SOIL   **NO DIG SOIL**

AGGREGATION INCREASES IN NO DIG SOIL

Under a microscope (x400), soil samples from my dig and no dig trial beds (see p.29) appear quite different. No dig soil contains larger aggregates, while the dig soil is mainly smaller mineral particles, even though the same amount of compost is added to each bed annually.

MYTH-BUSTING
NO DIG DOES NOT NEED MORE COMPOST

Perhaps because I've been so eager to promote the use of compost, many gardeners mistakenly believe that no dig beds need a thicker compost mulch than those that are dug or forked over. This is not the case. My trials show that when the same amount of compost is applied to dig and no dig beds, no dig gives bigger harvests.

Comparison from my trial beds

For 11 years now, I have applied the same amount of compost to two adjacent 5x16ft (1.5x5m) beds and planted them with identical vegetable crops. The only difference between them is that one has the compost dug into the soil, while the other is no dig with the compost on its surface. Every year, I weigh and record the harvests from each bed (see p.30). After 11 years, the dig bed has yielded 2,276lb (1,032kg) of vegetables and the no dig bed has produced 2,577lb (1,169kg). That's quite a difference from the same amount of compost! These results show that to produce a given amount of food, gardeners using no dig methods need a smaller area and therefore less compost.

An initial boost for soil

One source of confusion may be that I start no dig beds with a large dose of compost, 4–6in (10–15cm) thick. This is a one-off boost, and every year after that they are spread with a modest 1in (2.5cm) layer of compost, which is very much in line with traditional compost use.

This initial investment in more compost is optional. I consider it worthwhile, because it delivers an almost instant improvement in growing conditions, which lasts for many years as the organic matter is broken down and soil life is enhanced (see pp.19–21). It can quickly take your gardening to the next level by reducing the need for weeding, improving moisture retention, and providing better drainage. Over the years, I've also come to appreciate that highly bred vegetables are demanding plants, and if you want good results, it really pays to get more organic matter onto the soil to provide the best possible growing conditions.

HARVESTS FROM DIG AND NO DIG TRIAL BEDS

Every year, I plant twice—in spring and early to midsummer—and weigh and record the harvests. Both beds receive the same compost, but the no dig bed is consistently more productive.

- Dig bed yield (lb/kg)
- No dig bed yield (lb/kg)

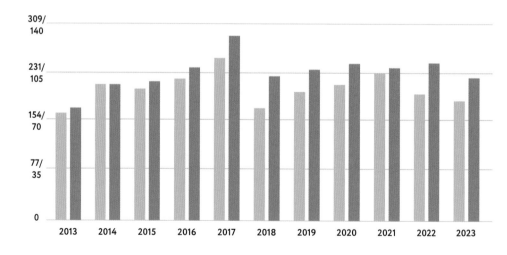

MULCHING AND NO DIG
REDUCE WEEDS

Plants viewed by gardeners as weeds are adept at colonizing empty ground very rapidly, their tenacious roots binding disturbed soil together to help it heal. Both mulching with compost and avoiding digging break this cycle of soil disturbance and healing, calming weed growth, and making weeding much easier and quicker.

Effects combine to give fewer weeds

I've observed that even an annual 1in (2.5cm) application of compost on no dig beds results in a remarkable reduction in weed growth. One reason I recommend using a thick 4–6in (10–15cm) compost mulch when you start no dig beds is to help smother existing weeds by excluding light, but the thin layer applied in subsequent years is not enough to have the same effect. It has been suggested that the boost that compost gives soil microbial life can help inhibit weeds. Research has shown that the presence of mycorrhizal fungi (see p.24) suppresses the growth of aggressive agricultural weeds, but the influence of the soil microbiome on weed germination remains largely unexplored.

What is clear is that fewer weed seeds germinate where soil is undisturbed thanks to no dig. This is because soil contains a store of dormant seeds that will take the opportunity to germinate as soon as they're brought to the surface by digging–if you don't dig, they can't grow!

Good gardening is still essential

Even with no dig, however, weeds will still blow in or germinate from seeds in compost, which means it is important to keep on top of weeds all the time. Being diligent and weeding little and often catches small weeds before they can set seed or spread, preventing them from multiplying and becoming overwhelming.

The best way to control weeds while minimizing soil disturbance is to watch for their tiny seed leaves as they germinate. As soon as they are visible, run a sharp hoe through the surface layer of compost to cut and disturb their roots. Do this on a dry, sunny day, and seedlings will rapidly shrivel and die. Larger weeds, especially perennials that can regrow from long, thick roots, can be removed individually using a hand fork or trowel. Where it is difficult to remove deep roots, quickly remove any new shoots that grow from them as they appear through the surface before they produce leaves to feed the roots below.

❝ Weed roots are much easier to extract from the soft, crumbly compost of a no dig bed than from sticky soil. ❞

COMMERCIALLY AVAILABLE MULCHES

It is fine to buy compost to supplement your own supply. This is especially true when starting out, but I regularly use commercial composts to mulch soil, as well as for propagation. Choose a product that is suited to your task and that is fit for your purpose.

Options for mulching

Materials that are ideal for use as mulches generally have a fairly coarse texture and contain plenty of organic matter, with varying levels of nutrients and microbial life. Watch out for contaminants, such as plastic or glass. Beware also of compost that is still hot, as this means it is still actively decomposing and not ready for use–often the case with green waste compost.

Herbicide contamination in manure

Pyralid weedkillers, sometimes sprayed on grass used for horse hay, are not broken down by composting and can harm garden plants where the contaminated compost is used. Test for pyralids by sowing fava beans into small pots of compost. Seeds won't germinate if contamination is serious, or will grow weakly with new leaves turning inward in lower concentrations.

MULCH	DESCRIPTION	POSITIVES	NEGATIVES
GREEN WASTE COMPOST	Waste from private gardens mostly, shredded and composted rapidly in huge, hot heaps	Low price, weed-free, readily available	Little microbial life, not rich in nutrients, often contains plastic
MUSHROOM COMPOST	Spent compost from mushroom growing, made from straw, manure, and small amounts of chalk and peat	Good nutrient status, weed-free, microbial life, pleasant to use, roughly neutral pH	Higher price, possible contamination with antibiotics
ANIMAL MANURES	Dung from horses or cows, usually combined with bedding materials, like straw or wood chips. Compost before use to prevent nutrient leaching	Good nutrient status, microbial life, often cheap where readily available	May contain contaminants, including plastic, glass, antibiotics, or herbicides (see opposite)
BIODIGESTATE	Not compost, but plant material or animal manure that has undergone anaerobic digestion by bacteria. Use with caution.	Weed-free	Low population of microbes, doesn't break down on soil surface, attracts slugs

OTHER USES FOR HOMEMADE COMPOST

Homemade compost can also be used for propagation in small pots or modules. A fine texture is important here, so it needs to be well decomposed and not too wet. The best results are from compost that is 8 to 12 months old, with a crumbly and even structure.

Sowing seed and repotting

Homemade compost is a brilliant option for sowing seeds and raising young plants, especially since the quality of so much commercial compost has decreased as suppliers struggle to find consistently good alternatives to peat. I currently combine around one part homemade compost with one part bought multipurpose compost (reliable brands that are dense and full of nutrition), with great results. For sowing small seeds, I may add one part sifted composted wood chips, sand, vermiculite, or perlite.

There is a worry that seeds will not grow well in compost containing too many nutrients, but this is unfounded. The nutrients and beneficial microbes in homemade compost allow seedlings to put on strong and healthy growth, including in tiny modules or small pots. I find this produces sturdy young plants that are ready to plant outdoors, sometimes as little as two or three weeks after sowing.

Your compost's structure may be too dense to provide good drainage in larger pots, so it is best lightened with about 10 percent finely sifted composted wood chips, sand, vermiculite, or perlite. If you have a wormery, up to 10 percent worm compost is a

welcome addition to a compost mix for its fine texture, fertility, and microbes. The presence of weed seeds can be a worry, but you can take steps to keep them to a minimum in your compost (see pp.68–69). I find it quick and easy to remove any weed seedlings from my potting compost as I notice them growing.

Filling raised beds

When creating a new bed with compost, especially in dry conditions, tamp it down before planting so roots can anchor well. It is often said that raised beds shouldn't be filled with compost alone, because it breaks down and loses too much volume. I would flip this around and say it's an advantage that the level sinks, because it gives you the opportunity to add some new compost every year. As time passes, compost gradually decomposes further and becomes more dense, so the loss of volume each year is smaller.

SEED SOWING MIX

A simple 1:1:1 mix of homemade and multipurpose composts, with composted wood chips, vermiculite, perlite, or sand to aid drainage, works well for sowing small seeds.

Homemade
compost

Bought, multipurpose
compost

Sifted composted wood chips/
vermiculite / perlite / sand

IDEAL POTTING MIX

For general potting, a mix of homemade compost and wood chips is good. Worm compost adds extra fertility and structure, if it is available.

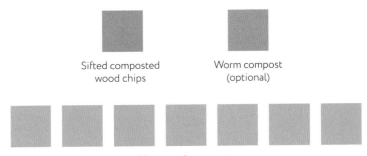

Sifted composted
wood chips

Worm compost
(optional)

Homemade compost

Chapter 2

How composting works

THE BASIC PRINCIPLES

Gathering materials together in a compost heap speeds
up the natural processes of decomposition to break down
organic material quickly and evenly. A basic understanding
of how decomposition occurs is all you need to make a start
and compost with confidence.

Create conditions for composting organisms to thrive

A productive compost heap is alive with its own ecosystem.
Organisms from microscopic bacteria and fungi to worms
and woodlice quickly arrive to feed on a heap's organic
material. In order to convert garden and kitchen waste into
compost, they need to breed and flourish in favorable living
conditions. Learning to provide for their needs is a vital part
of successful composting.

These microbes and other composting organisms need
three things: food, air, and moisture. The skill of composting
is to provide these in amounts that create a balance. Keep a
heap's conditions stable by adding a mixture of high-nitrogen,
and often moist, "green" materials to feed bacteria and drier,
more fibrous "brown" materials, which feed fungi and retain
air within the heap (see pp.64–65).

Signs of successful decomposition

A clear sign that composting is underway is a decrease in the volume of material in a heap. This may be rapid and quite dramatic after you add large amounts of green and brown materials. It happens because decomposers—mainly bacteria—are eating the fibers of materials, causing them to collapse.

Heat is generated by the metabolic activity of bacteria as they convert food into energy. Larger heaps can hold and breed more bacteria, so they tend to generate more heat, but smaller heaps can also noticeably warm up after a large addition of new material. Watch for water vapor rising from a heap on a cool morning, feel for warmth with your hand, or get a more accurate temperature measurement using a compost thermometer (see p.128).

Delve inside a heap, and where there is decomposition, you'll notice that the materials become a darker color and more homogeneous. Slender white threads of fungal or bacterial growth may also be visible. Later, you will find red tiger worms, one indicator of compost being ready to use (see pp.85–86).

66 The volume of material in a heap often decreases rapidly after you add large amounts of green and brown waste. **99**

THE SCIENCE OF SUCCESSFUL COMPOSTING

A more detailed look at what's happening inside your compost heap reveals that different organisms dominate as decomposition progresses. These transitions are caused by changes in temperature and sources of food. An awareness of them can help you follow and manage the process in your own heap.

Why encourage bacterial decomposition?

Bacteria are tiny, single-celled organisms that surround us in nature and are everywhere in our bodies. They are certainly present in any compost heap, where we can create conditions that allow them to multiply and speed up the composting process. Bacteria eat and breed extremely quickly, so, even when starting a heap from scratch, decomposition will be underway within hours if you add a good quantity of material in small pieces containing at least 50 percent of the nitrogen-rich "greens" in which they thrive. Grass clippings are the best example of this.

The heat generated by bacterial activity helps break down soft materials and speed up decomposition, potentially with the added benefit of killing weed seeds and any disease-causing microbes if temperatures exceed about 131°F (55°C). When this fast bacterial decomposition takes place, it is the first stage of quite a rapid process that will create compost within four to nine months, allowing you to process more organic materials and quickly provide top-quality food for your soil life.

The contribution of fungi

Most fungi are multicelled organisms and are slower than bacteria to break down organic materials. Heaps where small amounts of materials are added, or where the majority of food sources are carbon-rich "browns," do not support vigorous bacterial growth and will rely on fungi to produce compost more slowly. Fungi have the ability to access nutrients in woody plant material and brown fall leaves by producing powerful enzymes capable of breaking down tough lignin and cellulose. This time-consuming process does not generate heat and results in a wonderful rich compost. It is fungal decomposition that produces leaf mold and the half-composted wood chips that I find so useful for mulching paths (see p.124).

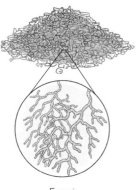

GREEN MATERIALS   **BROWN MATERIALS**

Bacteria   Fungi

MICROORGANISMS INVOLVED IN DECOMPOSITION
Bacteria need a diet rich in nitrogen from "green" compostable materials. Fungi are able to break down tough, carbon-rich "brown" materials.

PHASES OF DECOMPOSITION

The composting process is not uniform and usually happens in several phases as changes in temperature and food sources are exploited by successions of different decomposers.

1. Initial (mesophilic) phase–several days

Where a sufficient volume of green matter is added, bacteria will thrive and multiply rapidly, their activity gradually raising the temperature of the heap. Initially, these will be "psychrophilic" (cold-loving) and then "mesophilic" (medium heat) bacteria, which will actively feed on and decompose material until temperatures reach about 55°F (13°C) and 104°F (40°C) respectively.

This graph shows temperature fluctuations and changes in microbial activity during the different phases of decomposition.

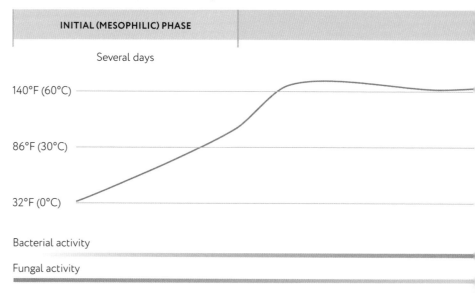

INITIAL (MESOPHILIC) PHASE

Several days

140°F (60°C)

86°F (30°C)

32°F (0°C)

Bacterial activity

Fungal activity

2. Hot (thermophilic) phase—up to 2 months, depending on additions

In a busy heap, there is enough bacterial metabolism for the temperature to rise higher than 104°F (40°C), creating conditions where "thermophilic" (heat-loving) bacteria can breed rapidly. This initiates the "hot phase" of composting, when a heap can reach 131–158°F (55–70°C)—hot enough to kill weed seeds. Huge numbers of thermophilic bacteria rapidly consume the remaining green materials, causing the heap to shrink in volume. The heat generated is temporary, lasting just a few days, unless either the heap is very large or new green materials are regularly added to fuel further bacterial activity.

HOT (THERMOPHILIC) PHASE

Up to 2 months

3. Cooling phase–1 to 2 months

Once temperatures have fallen, mesophilic bacteria return
to continue decomposition, and fungi move in to feed on the
fibrous and woody materials that remain. The volume of the
heap continues to decrease, but more slowly than during
the hot phase.

In heaps containing predominantly woody materials,
this fungal phase is the main driver of decomposition. Woody
materials become high-quality compost, just more slowly without
the heat from thermophilic bacteria, and with the possibility of
surviving weed seeds. Lots of bulky, brown materials mean that
the reduction in volume is less dramatic than in heaps with lots
of bacterial decomposition.

COOLING PHASE

1 to 2 months

140°F (60°C)

86°F (30°C)

32°F (0°C)

Bacterial activity

Fungal activity

4. Reheating after turning–1 month

If you are able to turn your heap (see pp.83–84), the best moment to do it is toward the end of the cooling phase. There is often still some warmth in the heap at this stage, with temperatures hovering around 86–95°F (30–35°C), but there will also be increased fungal activity and a few worms arriving to feed on material at the edges, where it's cooler.

Turning, or any kind of moving or mixing of the materials on the heap, introduces oxygen and makes new food available to bacteria. Their increased activity can cause heat to increase to around 140°F (60°C) again in larger heaps and helps ensure all materials are decomposed more uniformly.

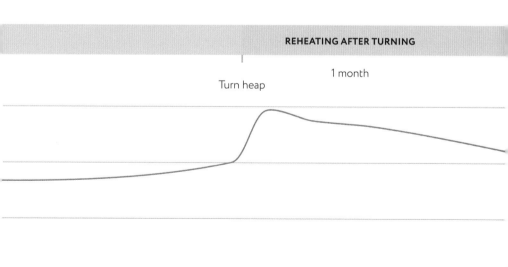

REHEATING AFTER TURNING

1 month

Turn heap

5. Maturing phase–1 to 2 months

Once fungi colonize the heap, it continues to lose heat and becomes an attractive home for many invertebrates, which arrive and breed rapidly. Red tiger worms (*Eisenia fetida*) love to feed on this partially decomposed organic matter and are often found in large numbers at this stage. Woodlice (*Oniscidea*) also move in to feed on woody material as it breaks down. During this "maturing" or "ripening" phase, composting happens at a more leisurely pace and the heap continues to slowly reduce in volume. There is no "end point" of this last phase; instead, it's your choice when you want to use the compost, which need not be perfect looking (see pp.85–86).

MATURING PHASE

1 to 2 months

140°F (60°C)

86°F (30°C)

32°F (0°C)

Bacterial activity

Fungal activity

MYTH-BUSTING
WORMS ARE NOT VITAL

Many different species of worms live in gardens, and they feed
and behave in different ways. This causes confusion, and composting
worms are often referred to as earthworms, which they are not!

Not the only decomposers

Don't expect to find the long, pink earthworms (*Lumbricus
terrestris*) in a compost heap. They burrow deep into soil and
come to the surface at night to pull down organic material to feed
on. Composting or red worms, mainly *Eisinia fetida*, are smaller
and redder. They live in and feed on decaying organic materials
in surface leaf litter, vegetable waste, compost heaps as they cool,
or in a dedicated wormery, where they can breed rapidly.

Red worms often become numerous in heaps with plenty of
moisture. When they arrive, they are visibly busy in a heap, but a
huge supporting crew of unseen decomposers also breaks down
material. Bacteria, fungi, and other microbes actually carry out
most decomposition in compost heaps. This means you can make
good compost without worms, so don't worry if they're not
around and don't feel you need to buy worms to add to a heap.

Worms come and go during composting

The heat generated by bacterial activity in a heap (see p.44)
creates temperatures higher than worms can cope with. Above
about 79°F (26°C), they migrate to a heap's edges or base–or even
into the soil below–and return when it's cooled. I see red worms
in moist heaps where compost has cooled and is maturing.

FEEDING FUELS
DECOMPOSITION

Microbes spearhead the decomposition process, but
compost heaps also host an incredible array of more complex
organisms. These consume and help break down the
abundant organic materials and also prey on each other.

A diversity of decomposers

Organisms that eat fresh (recently alive) organic materials are
called primary consumers, but they may be active at any stage in
the composting process where suitable food is present. These
include bacteria and fungi, but also microscopic nematode
worms, mites, woodlice, and millipedes. Slugs play a useful role,
too, as most species feed on the dead plant material found in a
compost heap instead of healthy garden plants. Any slugs a heap
attracts arrive to feast on the regular supply of decaying
vegetation they find there and won't cause an increase in slug
damage to your plants. Red tiger worms are voracious consumers
of partly decomposed material and often arrive and breed rapidly
during compost's "maturing" phase (see p.50).

Predators and prey

Secondary consumers feed on the primary consumers and are
invertebrates such as springtails, nematodes, and some species
of beetle. Finally, tertiary consumers are larger invertebrates—
such as ground beetles, centipedes, and ants—that prey on the
secondary consumers. You may also notice frogs, toads, and mice
at the edges of heaps, where they find welcome food and shelter.

AEROBIC vs. ANAEROBIC DECOMPOSITION

Air is a vital ingredient in the composting mix if you want to produce sweet-smelling, crumbly compost that is pleasant to handle. Decomposition is possible without air, but the foul smells and slimy results make it something most gardeners are eager to avoid.

What difference does air make?

The bacteria responsible for aerobic decomposition in a compost heap need oxygen to convert food into energy. Where air is present, they will decompose organic materials rapidly and with few unpleasant odors.

Anaerobic bacteria are found where there is little or no oxygen. Extracting energy from the organic material they feed on without oxygen produces foul-smelling gases like hydrogen sulfide and ammonia. Anaerobic decomposition is slower and smellier and results in soggy compost, often containing putrefied material.

Causes of anaerobic conditions

Anaerobic decomposition is common in wet compost heaps. Excess water seeps into pores between materials, displacing the air that's essential for aerobic bacteria to survive. This can happen when rainwater falls into an uncovered heap or if too many soft, moist green materials are added without dry, brown materials to provide structure and absorb excess moisture (see pp.72–73). Anaerobic conditions might be found through an entire heap or in patches. Large heaps can also become anaerobic at their center where air has been pushed out by the weight of the materials above. The clue is always that unmistakably swampy, sulfurous smell.

Remedies for a smelly compost heap

Squeeze a handful of a heap's contents: if water seeps out, it is too wet. The best remedy is to turn the whole heap (see pp.83–84). Air can also be introduced by mixing the contents using a fork or an aerator tool (see p.129). Anaerobic compost can be spread on soil in a thin layer, exposing it to air so it continues to break down aerobically.

HOW TO AVOID ANAEROBIC CONDITIONS

Add only small to medium volumes of green materials in one go and layer them with fibrous browns to absorb moisture and create spaces for air.

Place a drain pipe in the center of larger heaps and remove it once filling is finished to allow air to enter as gases escape.

Do not add water unless new materials are mostly dry.

Put a lid on heaps that are full of material and maturing to keep out rainwater.

MYTH-BUSTING
HEAT IS NOT ESSENTIAL

The phrase "hot composting" causes a buzz when it's claimed that you need only a few weeks to create high-quality, ready-to-use compost. This is not always true and gives the impression that heat generated by bacteria during the decomposition process is a vital part of making good compost. Let's check this out.

How temperatures rise

Heat is an optional part of the composting process, and it won't occur if you're not adding sufficient volumes of green materials (see p.72). This means that small heaps tend to heat up less than large ones and do not maintain a raised temperature because of their smaller volume. Green materials contain the nitrogen that feeds heat-generating bacteria, so compost heaps in winter heat up less because there are fewer green materials available.

The question of speed

Raised temperatures accelerate decomposition, but there is no reason why we have to make compost really fast. Some bins, like hot boxes (see pp.105–107), contain insulation designed to retain heat and can speed up decomposition but are expensive and not vital for success. In contrast, wormeries rely on the hard work of worms instead of bacteria to yield compost fast without heat.

At the other end of this spectrum, leaf mold takes up to two years to break down in a heap that never warms up (see p.95).

IMPACT OF HEAT ON THE SPEED OF COMPOSTING

Composting methods that generate more heat tend to
be faster, but cool composting also gives great results.

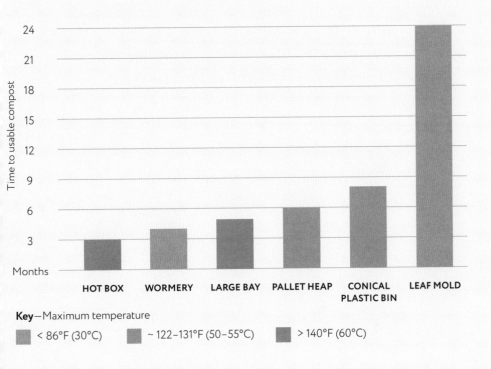

Key—Maximum temperature

- ▓ < 86°F (30°C)
- ▓ ~ 122–131°F (50–55°C)
- ▓ > 140°F (60°C)

Slow compost like this is dominated by decomposing fungi,
which take their time to break down tougher, woodier materials,
but the resulting product is rich in fungal life, great for soil
health, and well worth the wait. So if you have a small garden or
little green waste, don't be put off composting. You can relax in
the knowledge that your compost will be of high quality—it will
just take a while longer to break down.

EVERY HEAP IS DIFFERENT

Composting is so interesting and joyful because the results are
different every time. I'm still learning after 45 years! With each new
heap, you can experiment to find the best ways to produce compost
of the quality you want using the materials you can source.

Monitor moisture levels

Moisture causes more angst among composters than anything
else, because material can't decompose if it's dry or turns
anaerobic and smelly (see pp.54–55) if it's too wet. Most moisture
within a heap comes from the materials' inherent water content.
Kitchen peelings tend to be wet, while fall leaves and woody
prunings are drier. Recent weather is also a big influence, with
more water in lush, wet leaves and stems than in similar green
leaves during a drought. You can maintain a desirable moisture
level by adding a mix of different materials of varied
characteristics (see pp.64–65) and, if materials are very dry,
by adding water to the heap with a watering can (see p.77).

Quantity counts

The amount of material added to a heap is the main variable that influences how fast compost decomposes (see p.56). When additions are small, even if regular, bacterial breakdown is slow. The heap won't get hot, yet this can still result in nice compost (see pp.94–95). In contrast, large additions of fresh materials enable rapid multiplication of bacteria, and decomposition is much faster. It helps to have the right-sized bin for your quantity of materials (see pp.92–93), because a full smaller bin produces compost more quickly than a larger one where materials are spread thinly.

Seasonal variations

There will be more green material from spring to fall, when plants are in growth and the garden is busy, and generally very little of them during winter. While these moist green resources predominate in spring and summer, drier brown materials become more common in fall and winter (see pp.73–75). Collecting and then saving brown materials in winter to add during summer is a useful way to balance additions.

66 Your compost heaps will differ depending on the time of year. **99**

Chapter 3

What to compost and how to do it

WHAT CAN YOU COMPOST?

In my experience, almost all garden waste; kitchen peelings; and materials manufactured from plants, like paper and cardboard, can be composted. There's a lot of confusing and sometimes misleading information out there about what should not be added to a heap.

Composting need not be complicated

Keep things simple and save time by adding all your plant-based waste materials except any wood you're unable to chop or shred. There is no need to separate out so-called "undesirable" materials. This gives a greater amount of usable waste, which produces more compost in a shorter time through the extra volume and greater warmth generated (see p.58).

Take a thoughtful approach

If there is no sensible reason why something shouldn't be composted, then keep adding it to your heap. I find only beneficial effects from composting weeds, diseased plant material, egg shells, and citrus peels (see pp.66–71). Avoid only synthetic materials such as plastics, because they are not broken down by the composting process. Watch out for plastic labels on fruit, in brown paper tape, interwoven in teabags, and hidden between layers of some cardboard.

The meaning of "organic"

The word "organic" means any material derived from living organisms, whether plants or animals. It is often used to describe types of waste that are suitable for composting, and it does not mean that what goes into your compost has to have been grown "organically." It should also be noted that any compost can be labeled for sale as "organic" because it is made from organic matter; this term does not tell you anything further about the materials it contains.

Microorganisms can break down toxins

I am confident that edible and ornamental plants grown using most pesticides and herbicides can be added to a heap, along with paper and cardboard manufactured using industrial processes, because composting microbes have an almost magical ability to break down many toxic substances. An important exception to this are persistent pyralid herbicides (see p.34)

This detoxification of materials by microorganisms is known as "bioremediation." The work of the mycologist Paul Stamets showing that enzymes produced by fungi can degrade and reduce the toxicity of crude oil is one striking example of this. If microbes can break down oil spills successfully, then they'll have no problems degrading any low levels of pesticides or chemical residues that may be present in your domestic waste. The countless beneficial bacteria and fungi involved in the process of decomposition are responsible for remarkable transformations, even in an ordinary garden compost heap, providing a sustainable way to deal with waste materials and produce a really valuable end product.

❝ If there is no sensible reason why something shouldn't be composted, then keep adding it to your heap. ❞

CATEGORIZING MATERIALS

To make good compost, we need to understand the materials we have available and how best to use them. One helpful way to categorize compostable waste is into nitrogen-rich "green" materials and carbon-rich "brown" wastes, as these have quite different qualities and decompose at different rates.

Distinguishing green from brown

Greens are mostly moist and soft and speed up decomposition by providing food for bacteria in a heap. Browns are drier, originate from woody material, and make ideal food for fungi. They contain cellulose and lignin, which give woody plants their rigidity, and are more difficult for microorganisms to break down. It's no surprise then that tough browns are slower to decompose, and their presence maintains sufficient air in a heap for aerobic decomposition (see p.54) to result in sweet-smelling compost.

All compostable materials contain both nitrogen and carbon, and some—like brassica stalks and young green wood—have both green and brown qualities. Balancing the proportions of green and brown materials in your heap is the key to achieving great compost. I will describe how to create the right mix and why it's so important on pp.72–73.

GREEN

Green leaves and soft stems from ornamental and vegetable plants

Grass clippings

Weed leaves

Kitchen vegetable peelings and trimmings

Citrus peels

Coffee grounds

Fresh manure from plant-eating animals without bedding

Urine

Hair and animal fur

GREEN/BROWN

Green wood prunings from young growth of shrubs, trees, hedges, roses

Hay

Tough green stems, such as brassicas, sunflowers

Faded herbaceous perennial stems and leaves

Fresh manure with bedding

BROWN

Dry fallen leaves

Woody prunings

Paper and cardboard in small pieces

Wood chips

Straw

Egg shells

Wood ash

Soil

Old compost/poor-quality purchased compost

MYTH-BUSTING
YOU CAN COMPOST THAT!

Taking a positive approach has led me to discover that almost all garden waste can be composted safely and successfully. This increases the volume of waste you can add and the heap's temperature—two big positives. Relax and trust the decomposing microbes to work their magic.

Rhubarb leaves and citrus peels

Possibly because they are naturally acidic, I often see cautions about composting rhubarb leaves and citrus peels, yet both can be added to your heap without any adverse effects. Rhubarb leaves contain oxalic acid, which in high concentrations can be poisonous to mammals, birds, and even some insects. That does not make it toxic to microbes in a compost heap, however, which will naturally break it down into harmless organic molecules.

Adding a range of different materials to a heap will tend to balance out its pH. In addition, there is little need to worry about the pH of your finished compost, because it's highly unlikely to change the soil pH. You will know this if you have grown acid-loving plants, like rhododendron or blueberries, in neutral or alkaline soil; even after the addition of a 12in (30cm) layer of acidic compost on soil, its pH reverts to alkaline within a few years. No dig gardeners apply around 1in (2.5cm) of compost annually (see p.29), and the microbes in healthy no dig soil help maintain the soil pH around plant roots.

Perennial weed roots

Perennial weeds are those that can regrow year after year from their fleshy roots. Often, even small sections of their roots that remain in soil after weeding or digging will send up shoots, which makes gardeners wary of adding them to compost heaps. I add them to a heap without any preparatory treatment, because all perennial weed roots will decompose, even in a cool heap, as long as they can't reach light.

Keep the contents of a heap in darkness by lining the inside of any slatted sides (see p.98) and by closing the plastic lids of smaller compost bins. In a heap cooler than about 86°F (30°C), decomposition might take eight weeks. Higher temperatures will cause roots of couch grass and bindweed to break down and disappear within four weeks.

I have successfully composted bindweeds (*Convolvulus arvensis* and *Calystegia sepium*), couch grass (*Elymus repens*), ground elder (*Aegopodium podagraria*), dandelion (*Taraxacum officinale*), docks (*Rumex* spp.)–although if the roots are large, I would cut them into pieces–stinging nettles (*Urtica dioica*), and creeping buttercup (*Ranunculus repens*). I have never needed to compost horsetail (*Equisetum arvense*), but I would add it to heaps if it were in my garden.

Weed seeds

Even just a day or two above 122–131°F (50–55°C) is enough to kill weed seeds. Such warmth is most likely at the center of a heap, so that's where seedheads should be placed. The seeds not only of weeds but also of all sorts of other plants, like tomatoes and squashes, can survive a cool composting process to germinate after the compost is spread. This can look like a difficult problem but actually is not at all.

The benefits of using homemade compost (see pp.16–18) mean it's worth accepting the presence of some weed seeds. This is easy thanks to no dig (see p.8), where the soft compost remains on the soil surface and any seedlings can quickly be dealt with as soon as they are seen. Except in winter, allow 7–10 days after spreading compost for weed seeds to germinate before lightly raking or running a hoe through the compost on a dry day. This kills germinating seedings and leaves the surface clear for sowing and planting. Don't sow carrots on the day you spread the compost!

Diseased material

I add all diseased plant material to my heaps, even those that don't get hot, and I observe no ill effects when compost is spread on the soil. This advice is contrary to common gardening beliefs, but there are good reasons why it works. First, many (though not all) diseases are a natural part of the decomposition process. Mildews, for example, appear toward the end of a plant's growth cycle and speed decomposition of older leaves. Very few fungal or bacterial pathogens can survive on dead plant material, and all will be killed in a hot compost heap.

Even if pathogens did survive, disease would not be spread with the compost, because specific diseases need specific conditions to infect plants. The fungal spores that cause these diseases will already be floating in the air, ready to infect vulnerable plants when the season or weather allow. For example, cucurbit plants are prone to powdery mildew in late summer when their fruits are grown, while tomatoes and potatoes are susceptible to infection by airborne spores of late blight only in warm, wet summer weather.

" Perennial weed roots will decompose, even in a cool heap, as long as they cannot reach light. **"**

Conifers

Branch prunings and needles from conifers make good additions to a compost heap when chopped up small, like all woody materials (see p.76). They are acidic, but this low pH is mostly balanced by other waste materials and is not harmful to decomposing microbes. Conifer prunings also contain oils and resins, including terpenoids and phenolic compounds, which gives them a characteristic aroma that will be familiar if you have ever cut a conifer hedge or bought a sack of chipped bark. These compounds act to slow decomposition, but their impact is minimal when mixed with other organic materials.

Fallen fall leaves

Dry, brown tree leaves contain a lot of cellulose, which makes them almost woody and means they take longer to decompose than many other garden waste materials. Many people worry about undecomposed leaves in their finished compost, but in moderate amounts, they are a brilliant addition to any heap. Just be sure to balance their high carbon content with sufficient green materials. Speed up their decomposition by chopping leaves with a rotary lawnmower before adding to the heap.

If you collect many tree leaves, I recommend making a separate pile outdoors. This can be used as a source of brown material to balance the summer greens (see pp.73–75) or, if you have space, could be left to produce leaf mold (see p.124). Make sure leaves are fully moist and they will slowly decompose over two years in a fungal, slow manner.

COMPOSTABLE AND BIODEGRADABLE PACKAGING

Most paper and cardboard are ideal additions, but avoid any with a glossy finish and ensure that any plastic tape and labels are removed before adding to your heap. Don't assume that because a bag or carton is labeled "compostable" or "biodegradable" that it will break down at the same speed as other waste on your compost heap.

I have found that "compostable" plastic bags simply turn into a squishy lump after six months in a hot domestic compost heap. The materials that these bags are made from are often designed to break down during high-temperature commercial composting processes, which makes them unsuitable for adding to an ordinary garden compost bin.

The term "biodegradable" simply means that a material will separate or break down into pieces (degrade) over an unspecified length of time—possibly many years longer than you expect to wait for finished compost. Don't assume packaging is suitable for composting because it is labeled biodegradable.

ACHIEVING THE RIGHT BALANCE

When I started gardening, 32 parts carbon to 1 part nitrogen was seen as the ideal ratio to aim for when making additions to a compost heap. But this requires precise knowledge of the chemical makeup of waste, which is intimidating and impractical. I prefer to categorize waste as either "brown" or "green" (see pp.64–65) so that it's easy to combine them in quantities that will promote aerobic decomposition (see p.54).

Keep additions in proportion

Adding three parts green waste to one part brown waste by volume is not a hard and fast rule, but it is a useful guideline to follow. Brown materials are generally so dense and fibrous that just a small amount is enough to balance and aerate the softer, moister greens, which quickly collapse as they decompose.

Spread all new additions in a level layer instead of throwing everything into the middle of a heap. It's then easier to portion things out evenly across the whole heap or bin, and you can assess visually without having to measure things out. Even if you have large amounts of bulky green material that includes a lot of air, add no more than a 2in (5cm) layer before spreading roughly ½in (1cm) of brown material on top. A thick layer of soft green grass clippings would quickly become compacted and airless, so layers of brown material help maintain small air pockets in the heap, which are essential for good decomposition.

Seasonal variation

Garden waste varies considerably with the seasons, from the almost exclusively "browns" of dry fallen leaves and woody prunings during late fall and winter, to abundant "greens" in spring and summer when grass clippings, weeds, and foliage are plentiful. Our challenge is to maintain a balance of green and brown materials throughout the year. Do this by stockpiling browns for use in summer. Fall tree leaves and wood chips can be kept outdoors in a heap or bags, and paper and cardboard are often readily available. Hedge clippings are another useful source of browns during summer—green in color but containing a fair proportion of woody material. In contrast, we can't stockpile greens in summer because they decompose so quickly. Winter greens include coffee grounds, urine, and fresh manure.

THE SIMPLE FORMULA FOR SUCCESS

Composting is so often overcomplicated. Just stick to roughly three times the volume of greens to browns for great results.

1 part brown material

3 parts green material

A TIMELINE OF THE COMPOSTABLE YEAR

The types and quantities of garden materials for composting vary in every plot but always share a pattern in the availability of greens and browns that's linked to changes in the seasons. An understanding of these variations helps achieve a good green–brown balance in your heap throughout the year.

Woody prunings

Grass clippings
Weeds
Veggie plant waste
Cut-back perennials
Deadheads

Woody prunings

Grass clippings
Weeds
Veggie plant waste
Cut-back perennials

SPRING (MAR–MAY)

SUMMER (JUN–AUG)

THINKING AHEAD AND SAVING MATERIALS

Many gardening tasks are seasonal, but some of the brown waste created during fall and winter can be saved to balance additions during spring and summer, when greens predominate.

 Brown materials

 Green materials

Fall leaves
Woody prunings

Veggie plant waste
Cut-back perennials
Grass clippings/Weeds

Woody prunings
Wood chips

Veggie plant waste/Weeds

FALL (SEP–NOV)

WINTER (DEC–FEB)

TIPS FOR SUCCESSFUL COMPOSTING

Experience has taught me that a few simple tricks make a notable difference to the quality of my compost. Investing a little more time and effort considering what to add and preparing materials enables the best performance of our microbe allies in the heap, and the resulting compost will be easy to handle and quick to spread.

Chop up long stems and sticks

Too many woody stems more than 6in (15cm) long create a lattice effect in a heap, where large air spaces lead to very slow decomposition. The resulting compost is also filled with long sticks and strands, making it uneven and difficult to handle.

Use a knife, pruning shears, rotary lawnmower, or shredder (see pp.126–127) to chop all woody material and tough, fibrous stems. The best results are from pieces 2–4in (5–10cm) or less, which allow green and brown materials to bed down in contact with one another. These also increase the woody waste's surface area for microbes to access and decompose. I use a knife to cleave tough brassica and sunflower stems down the middle lengthwise twice, creating slimmer lengths that are easy to cut up.

Working with wood chips

Wood chips from your own garden or local tree surgeons are a valuable source of brown material, but I recommend you avoid using freshly chipped wood in a heap of mixed materials. This is simply because, even in small chips, the tough wood takes longer to break down than other waste in the heap and will still be there in your finished compost. Instead, it's much better to compost wood chips that are already partially decomposed, having spent at least six months in a separate, damp heap (see p.124).

To avoid large woody pieces remaining in my finished compost, I remove them by running old wood chips down a 45-degree throw-through sieve before adding the resulting finer and partly decomposed material to the heap.

Managing moisture

In wetter climates like the UK, we rarely need to add water to compost heaps, because most green materials already contain so much moisture that too many of them will result in a soggy, anaerobic heap. With sufficient layers of brown materials, moisture levels are naturally about right. Adding dry browns can even soak up excess moisture. Paper or cardboard are particularly useful for this, so don't prewet them before adding.

By contrast, in dry climates or during exceptionally hot and dry summer weather, garden waste contains less moisture, and it's often necessary to water your heap. Add water using a can or hose with a fine rose with each addition of material that looks and feels dry. Stop adding water if weather conditions and materials become wetter.

OTHER ADDITIONS
TO CONSIDER

The supply of compostable materials is not limited to our own
gardens. Look around for other sources of waste materials, which
can help speed up the decomposition process and result in
more compost to use.

Extra materials from outside the garden

If you want more bacterial heat to kill weed seeds, then it can be
worth adding other people's green weeds and seeds! I accept my
neighbor's offer of thistles, and I'm always on the lookout for
additional wastes. See if you can scrounge some of the materials
in the table opposite to boost your compost heap.

Accelerants and other composting products

Some aspects of compost making have been commercialized, and
I see little value in products called accelerants. Decomposition
takes place naturally without the need for proprietary inputs.
Accelerants speed up composting by adding nitrogen, and
possibly microbes, which any gardener can easily do for free
by adding extra grass clippings or coffee grounds.

Buying worms for your heaps is also a waste of money,
because as soon as temperatures rise above around 86°F (30°C)—
as they will in any compost heap where you're adding green
waste—worms will migrate to the edge or die off. Worms are not
a vital part of the composting process described here, but they
arrive naturally during the later phase of composting, after
bacterial decomposition has occurred (see p.51). If you make
and run a wormery, things are different (see pp.109–111).

ADDITIONAL COMPOSTABLE MATERIALS

MATERIAL	DESCRIPTION	SOURCE	CATEGORY
OTHER PEOPLE'S WEEDS	Any unwanted annual or perennial plants, including roots and seeds	Neighbors, fellow allotment holders	Green waste
GRASS CLIPPINGS	From lawns, verges, and paths, where no weedkiller is used	Cutting any nearby grass, with the owner's permission	Green waste
SPENT HOPS	A byproduct of the brewing process	Local breweries or friends who brew their own beer	Green waste
COFFEE GROUNDS	Ground coffee beans once they have been used to make coffee	Often given away by coffee shops	Green waste
HEDGE PRUNINGS	Largely woody waste from trimming evergreen or deciduous hedges	Neighbors or friends	Brown waste
WOOD CHIPS	Small pieces of wood created when branches of trees and shrubs are fed into a chipper	Tree surgeons, or local sources of woody waste if you have a chipper	Brown waste

WHEN TO STOP ADDING FRESH MATERIAL

It's possible to carry on adding small amounts of material to the top of a compost heap forever, because decomposition continually causes it to sink. But if you want a bay or bin full of usable compost that's evenly decomposed, you need to know when to stop adding to it.

Recognizing the right time

At what point should you stop adding new material? Unless you have a particularly large volume of materials to compost, it's usually possible to continue filling a heap for a whole year. However, I stop additions before a heap is crammed to the top, when it risks becoming compacted and airless at the bottom. If you're not sure, stop adding; otherwise, it is easy just to carry on and never reach an end point.

Where your bin or bay is the right size for the quantities of organic materials available (see pp.92–93), it should be possible to fill it sufficiently within two to three months between spring and fall. During winter, there will be hardly anything to add, and a heap is unlikely to reach the last addition point before spring arrives.

Why stop adding to your compost heap?

Where only one bin is continually added to, there will always be an undecomposed layer on top and a small but continuous supply of compost at the base, which can be removed and used. To finish one heap and start adding to a new one, two or more bins are needed.

The main reason to stop adding fresh materials is to have a heap entirely composed of maturing compost, in which all the contents can break down into a more homogeneous product, especially if the heap is turned (see opposite). This results in mature compost more quickly and means you can empty a larger volume of finished compost in one go, which is more useful for mulching bigger areas than occasional forkfuls from the base of a heap.

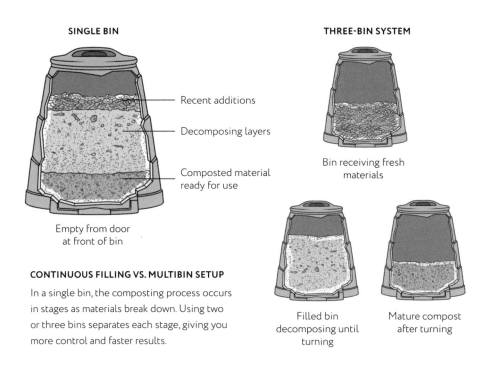

SINGLE BIN

Recent additions

Decomposing layers

Composted material ready for use

Empty from door at front of bin

THREE-BIN SYSTEM

Bin receiving fresh materials

Filled bin decomposing until turning

Mature compost after turning

CONTINUOUS FILLING VS. MULTIBIN SETUP

In a single bin, the composting process occurs in stages as materials break down. Using two or three bins separates each stage, giving you more control and faster results.

TO TURN OR NOT TO TURN?

Turning just means moving and shaking up the ingredients of a compost heap, but it probably causes more confusion than any other part of the process. After all, decomposition takes place without this intervention, so is turning really worth the effort?

The benefits of mixing it up, just once

Material at the drier, cooler edges of a heap tends to break down more slowly than what's in the warmer, moister center. Turning mixes these materials, breaking up any dry or soggy patches and creating a more evenly decomposed result. The process also provides fresh food for bacteria, often resulting in the heap warming up during a second round of decomposition (see p.49), which means that compost will be ready faster.

Turning can also rescue heaps that are anaerobic and smelly (see pp.54–55), as it's a chance to introduce more air, and mix dry material like paper into soggy patches. It is a straightforward way to massively improve your finished compost.

Different methods

A heap can be turned by physically moving it into an empty space, ideally a second empty bin or bay. I use a manure fork with long, thin prongs (see p.128). Add air to the material by shaking out any wet and dense lumps while mixing materials from the edges with those from the center. This physical task only needs to be done once per heap and is much easier if you can open bins or bays to provide good access to the waste.

Alternatively, use a turning tool, such as an aerator tool with a corkscrew design (see p.129). This mixes and aerates a heap without you having to empty it but is still hard work to use. Screw the tool downward from the top of the heap, then lift it up to bring material from the bottom to the top. Repeat this as the heap is filled.

When to turn

A heap is usually ready to turn one or two months after the last additions were made. Another indicator is to wait for a heap that has warmed up to 113–149°F (45–65°C) during decomposition to cool down to 68–95°F (20–35°C) before turning. It's not written in stone—just do it when you have the time. I find that the compost is ready two or three months after turning.

66 Turning is a straightforward way to speed up the process and massively improve your finished compost. **99**

WHEN IS COMPOST
READY TO USE?

When is it best to use compost, at what stage of decomposition? This question has no precise answer, because compost is continually breaking down. What's important is to consider how you plan to use the compost and to understand when it's ready for that purpose.

Don't look for perfection

Good homemade compost can be somewhat lumpy, with woody pieces still visible. This can make it appear unfinished when compared to bought compost, which is often finer because it has been chopped and sifted. But your compost doesn't have to look beautifully even and fully decomposed to have value in your garden. There is a balance to be struck between quality and quantity, especially if you are using compost as a mulch: waiting for "complete" decomposition results in much less volume. That said, compost for propagation needs a fine texture, and for that, I wait longer and accept that the heap will produce less.

How to decide when to spread

Deciding when compost is ready is your call, according to when your soil needs it and is free to receive a mulch layer. I mulch my no dig beds in late fall and, if necessary, will do this with compost that is less decomposed than I would prefer to ensure that soil life is fed and the soil is protected from winter rains, when there is no plant cover. This compost continues to break down on the surface so that it is mostly soft and fibrous by early spring when it's time to sow and plant.

As a rough rule of thumb, compost from an aerobic heap that you filled within three months (see p.81) can be used after six to eight months and should be very well decomposed after a year. Look for a roughly 50 percent reduction in volume, with enough decomposition that at least a half to three-quarters of the original materials are unrecognizable. A certain homogeneity and a dark brown color are good signs, as is the presence of red tiger worms (see p.50). Pieces of woody material will usually still be visible– you're not looking for everything to be fully decomposed.

If you have more compost than you need or are not ready to use it, then compost can be kept in a heap. Be aware though that stored compost will continue to decompose and lose volume, so the longer it's kept, the less you will have to spread.

" Compost doesn't have to look beautifully even and fully decomposed to have value in your garden. "

COMPOSTING BATHROOM WASTE

I have had a composting bathroom for nine years and have found that it is not just possible, but straightforward, to make good compost from human waste. It is a practical option and something that I encourage people to try.

My composting bathroom system

In this setup, designed by Dave Readman and built at Homeacres, a modified 6x8ft (1.8x2.4m) shed serves as a toilet for me, staff, and visitors. It is raised 1ft (30cm) above ground to provide more space for waste compartments underneath the floor. There are three seats inside, which enable some separation of pee and poop.

Underneath the seat reserved for pee, the compartment contains dry fibrous material such as hay or straw. Once this is wet, it is removed via an external door and is added to the compost heap, where its high nitrogen content makes it a material that's two-thirds green, and it decomposes very quickly.

There are two seats for poop, only one of which is in use at a time. After each visit to this seat, a handful of dry woody material, like sawdust or shredded paper, is added to absorb excess moisture, reduce the smell, and make a nice balanced compost material. After a year, that seat is shut down and the contents of the compartment below are left for a year to compost before they are emptied out and used. In the meantime, the second seat is used and the whole process is repeated.

SIDE ELEVATION 1

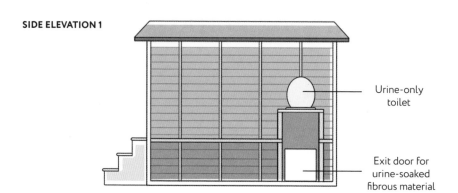

Urine-only toilet

Exit door for urine-soaked fibrous material

SIDE ELEVATION 2

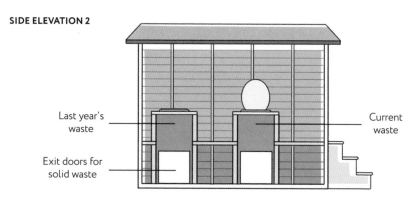

Last year's waste

Exit doors for solid waste

Current waste

OVERHEAD PLAN

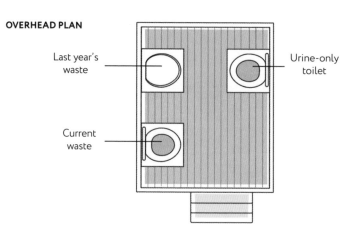

Last year's waste

Current waste

Urine-only toilet

Using the resulting compost

I'm pleasantly surprised by how crumbly and odor free the product from the composting bathroom is, but you don't get a lot—I reckon an average household would produce little more than three large wheelbarrows each year, depending partly on how much woody material is added.

When using the compost, think of it as animal manure. Well-composted waste is unlikely to harbor harmful bacteria, but it's best to be cautious and avoid using it around vegetable crops that will be eaten raw. I spread it around fruiting crops, roots, or leaves that will be cooked, and of course any ornamental plants. There are certainly some meat-eaters using the bathroom here, and I'm never aware of any problem with that. I think for most people on an average diet, this system would work very well.

HOMEACRES COMPOST BATHROOM

This is a simple way to achieve a rough separation of liquids and solids without using special separators. The urine-soaked material is emptied roughly once a month, and the solids once a year. Elevating the shed above ground level gives easier access when emptying waste compartments.

Chapter 4

Your composting setup

CHOOSING THE RIGHT SIZE HEAP FOR YOU

Everybody has different waste materials and different settings in which to deal with them. You might choose a bin inside your home for kitchen waste or build bays to deal with waste from a large, busy garden–there is no one–size–fits–all solution when it comes to composting. Finding the right fit for your own situation is the first step to success.

Quantity of waste determines heap size

It may come as a surprise to learn that small is beautiful when it comes to compost heaps! Have the smallest heap possible to enable you to fill it within a maximum of three months or, better still, two months during the growing season. A heap that is too big takes up more space; never fills up; and, because it doesn't heat up, will decompose very slowly.

If you are new to composting, you'll be amazed how material rapidly shrinks in volume as it decomposes. This is one reason why new gardeners often imagine they need a bigger heap than they actually do. Once you get the hang of adding ingredients in balance (see pp.72–73), decomposing bacteria will get to work and waste almost seems to disappear. This means that the amount of finished compost from a heap might be smaller than expected, but also that a heap can process a much greater volume of materials than you might anticipate. Therefore, a big heap is only ever needed in a large garden.

" Always bear in mind that the most effective results will come when you fill a heap within two or three months. "

Check the Visual guide to sizes and volumes (see pp.100–103) to help you work out which type of heap or bin would be the best fit for your space and the amount of compostable materials you have available. Taking the time to select what suits your needs will really pay off by making composting much quicker and easier.

COMPACT OPTIONS

In situations where only relatively small quantities of green garden and kitchen waste are available, consider enclosed composting methods, such as a hot box, a wormery, or bokashi bins (see pp.106–111). All of these take up less space than a conventional compost heap and can be placed in paved yards, on balconies, or even indoors.

COOL vs. HOT COMPOSTING

Heat is the answer if you're looking to produce the maximum amount of compost as quickly as possible, but it is not essential for decomposition to take place. Cool composting takes longer and does not kill weed seeds but is good for all other waste materials and results in excellent compost.

Advantages of hot composting

Decomposition is about three times faster in a hot heap compared to a cold one, meaning that materials might take six months instead of 18 months to break down (see right). It also then takes three times less space to compost the same quantity of materials.

A heap will only warm up if enough nitrogen-rich green waste is added to feed bacteria and allow them to rapidly multiply. It is possible for temperatures within a heap to rise above 122°F (50°C), and when they do, this speeds up the composting process, as well as killing weed seeds and potential pathogens. In large heaps, temperatures can even exceed 158°F (70°C), which is not desirable and gives blacker, denser compost. Adding brown materials, especially crumpled paper, helps bring the temperature down.

❝ Decomposition is about three times faster in a hot heap compared to cold composting. **❞**

How to stay cool

You can still make lovely compost without achieving heat, it just takes longer because it is mainly fungi instead of bacteria that will do the work of decomposition. Brown materials, such as fallen fall leaves or wood chips, molder slowly and surely to make beautiful compost (see p.124). The process might take two years though, which means you need sufficient space to leave them for longer.

Green waste can also decompose without heat in a wormery (see pp.109–111). This, however, is more demanding of your time, because worms are like pets that need constant management and feeding with material that has been chopped. The worms digest the waste, and their excretions (casts) are a wonderful fine compost that is excellent for plant propagation (see pp.36–39).

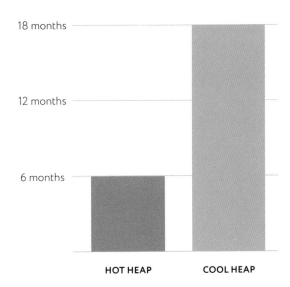

EFFECT OF TEMPERATURE ON COMPOSTING SPEED

Heat is not vital in a compost heap, but it does make a huge difference to the time it takes materials to break down into finished compost.

18 months

12 months

6 months

HOT HEAP   COOL HEAP

LOCATION AND ESSENTIAL FEATURES

Where and how you make a structure for composting will influence the outcome, as well as how easy it is to empty and use the resulting compost. There is conflicting advice out there that can make this confusing, but in reality there are just a few simple guidelines to follow.

A soil base is best

Soil is the ideal base for composting, because it allows excess moisture to drain away from decomposing materials. It also permits microbes and other organisms to enter and leave. Don't lay cardboard under a new heap to suppress weeds, because they will die anyway under the material being added. You can build a successful heap on concrete if there is a slight slope or gaps between flagstones for water to drain away.

Protection from the elements?

Neither sun nor shade is important for your compost heap; it can work well in either. Some kind of cover to keep rain out of finished heaps is worthwhile in wetter climates. I have a permanent roof over my large bays (see pp.120–123). My pallet bays are covered with sheets of corrugated iron while compost is maturing, but the heap being filled is left open for convenience.

Easy access

Good access is essential to make filling, turning, and emptying your heap hassle free. You will make hundreds of journeys to and from a heap while filling it with waste, which means a site near the middle of a larger garden is always worthwhile. Ensure there is room to maneuver a wheelbarrow if you use one.

Consider how you will access a heap's contents, either for turning or to remove finished compost. Small doors at the base of conical plastic bins (see p.106) are awkward to use and most people find access is easier either via the lid, or by lifting off the bin entirely. Pallet heaps can be made with wires securing each corner (see pp.114–117) so that it's only necessary to untwist two wires at one edge to access compost. Then you can swing open one pallet like a door. My big bay system (see pp.120–123) is constructed so that the boards can be unscrewed when we need access, which makes turning and emptying easier.

Building materials

Wood is strong and easy to work with, making it an ideal material to build compost bays. Always use untreated wood. This will shorten the structure's lifespan but avoids the risk of chemical contamination in your compost.

Use untreated wooden pallets, particularly avoiding anything labeled MB, which has been treated with toxic methyl bromide. Pallets probably won't last more than five years, but untreated wood is compostable once nails are removed. Buying untreated softwood is an expensive option, because it will only last a few years. I sourced Douglas fir to build my bays. This was worth the expense because it is naturally rich in oil and lasts much longer than most other softwoods without using any preservatives. Plywood is an easy way to make sides for a bin, but it's essential to check what type of resin glues have been used to adhere the thin sheets of wood together. If the resin is based on polyester, it decomposes within a year. However, if it's an epoxy resin–mainly used in marine plywood–it will not decompose for many years and is best avoided.

MYTH-BUSTING
SOLID SIDES ARE GOOD

An influential gardener and advocate of no dig methods in the mid-20th century called W. E. Shewell-Cooper instructed that, "The sides of a heap must be slatted to allow air to get in and circulate." This dictum has become entrenched in gardening practice, but if you stop and think about it, then air coming in from the sides of the heap is just going to cool the contents down and dry them out–it doesn't make sense!

The composting process works really well when the sides of a bin or bay are solid, not slatted. This is because they maintain moisture right to the edges of the heap and they retain the warmth generated by bacteria during decomposition. People worry about a lack of air resulting in anaerobic decomposition (see pp.54–55). However, the air that bacteria need is not drawn in from outside, but is already contained in the small gaps within a heap's structure that are created by additions of fibrous brown materials.

Conical plastic bins have solid sides and produce lovely compost in my garden. Bays made with pallets or with slatted wooden sides can simply be lined with cardboard. You can't line a whole bay in one go from bottom to top, because the cardboard gets wet and collapses. The simplest way is to slot pieces of cardboard boxes around the sides of a heap as it is filled. Then, when you eventually turn or use the heap, you have nice half-decomposed cardboard to add as brown material when you start a new heap.

A VISUAL GUIDE TO SIZES AND VOLUMES

It can be difficult to work out which composting bin or bay will fit your space and have the right capacity to hold the waste organic materials generated by your garden and household. This visual guide allows you to quickly compare the dimensions of different options, the volumes of material they can hold, and the amount of compost they're likely to produce.

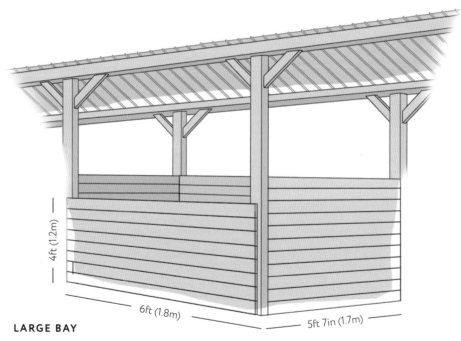

LARGE BAY

Volume when full of material 127ft³ (3.6m³)

Approx. volume of compost 60ft³ (1.7m³)

PALLET HEAP

Volume when full of material
42.4ft³ (1.2m³)

Approx. volume of compost
24.7ft³ (0.7m³)

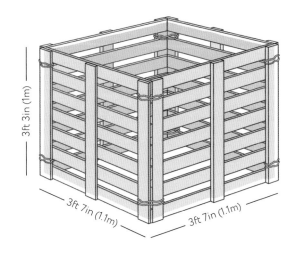

3ft 3in (1m)

3ft 7in (1.1m)

3ft 7in (1.1m)

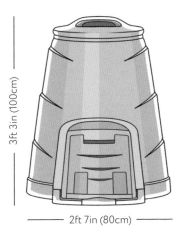

3ft 3in (100cm)

2ft 7in (80cm)

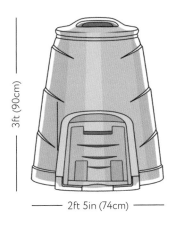

3ft (90cm)

2ft 5in (74cm)

CONICAL PLASTIC BIN (87-GAL/ 330 LITER)

Volume when full of material 11.7ft³ (0.33m³)

Approx. volume of compost 6.4ft³ (0.18m³)

CONICAL PLASTIC BIN (58-GAL/ 220-LITER)

Volume when full of material 7.8ft³ (0.22m³)

Approx. volume of compost 4.2ft³ (0.12m³)

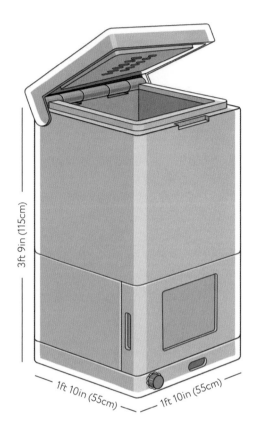

3ft 9in (115cm)

1ft 10in (55cm)

1ft 10in (55cm)

HOT BOX (SAMPLE 53-GAL/200-LITER, MANY DIFFERENT DESIGNS AVAILABLE)

Volume when full of material (Insulating walls 2in [5cm] thick, so take 4in [10cm] off each dimension measurement) 7.1ft³ (0.2m³)

Approx. volume of compost 3.9ft³ (0.11m³)

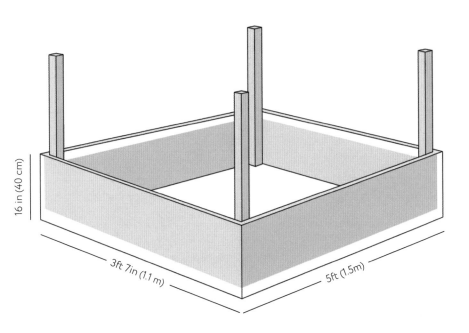

16 in (40 cm)

3ft 7in (1.1 m)

5ft (1.5m)

WORMERY

Height 16in (40cm) at peak, with sloping sides

Volume when full of material Regular small additions would never fill the wormery. Volume when at 16in (40cm) peak fill is 23.3ft³ (0.66m³)

Approx. volume of compost 14.1ft³ (0.4m³) after one year of small, regular additions

OPTIONS FOR SMALLER GARDENS

Composting can be tricky in small gardens, where space is at a premium and compostable materials are less varied and available only in smaller amounts. This makes it really important to choose a composting method that will suit your needs from the outset.

Types of waste

Think carefully about the materials that you will be composting. Your small garden may be packed with plants that could produce plenty of prunings and clippings that combine green and brown qualities (see pp.64–65) to fill a compost bin, along with some kitchen waste and shredded paper and cardstock. Or, if you grow a small quantity of annuals and vegetables and produce a good quantity of kitchen waste, then the bulk of what you compost would be green material, which may suit an alternative method, such as a wormery (see pp.109–111). Most composting bins suited to smaller gardens come in a variety of sizes, allowing you to choose one appropriate for the volume of materials you produce.

Be wary of gadgets and gimmicks

Many products exist that claim to make composting quicker, or easier, or to solve a composting "problem," such as unpleasant odors. Think carefully before buying what are often expensive items, because although they sound great, in my experience they solve very few potential issues. It's much better to gain some understanding of the composting process so you can run a simple setup efficiently and deal with any problems that might arise.

TYPE OF BIN	WASTE	BASE	LOCATION OPTIONS
CONICAL PLASTIC BIN	Mix of green and brown materials	Open base	Soil or free-draining hard surface
HOT BOX	Mix of green and brown materials	Closed base with stand	Soil or any hard surface, including patio or decking
BOKASHI	Food waste	Closed base	Usually indoors for convenience
WORMERY	Finely chopped green materials, including kitchen peelings	Free-standing kits: closed base with stand Raised bed enclosure: open base	Free-standing kits: outdoors on any level surface, sometimes indoors in freezing weather Raised bed enclosure: outdoors on soil

Conical plastic bins

My number-one option for composting garden and food waste in a smaller garden is a conical plastic bin. These are reasonably priced, widely available, and come in a standard 58-gallon (220-liter) size, with an 87-gallon (330-liter) model for slightly larger gardens. They are light and can easily be lifted to move around the plot and to access the contents for turning and emptying. Set up two or three and it's possible to run a good system, with one heap being filled and compost maturing in the others.

These bins are best positioned on soil and are very easy to use—just add layers of green and brown material to fill (see pp.64–65). The plastic walls and lid hold moisture inside the bin, so it's especially important to add brown material, like cardboard and prunings, to hold structure and air in the heap and stop it from becoming soggy and anaerobic (see pp.54–55). In summer, when green material is plentiful, the contents of a conical plastic bin can generate useful heat. The solid walls also help insulate the bin's contents and retain this heat for longer.

It's easy to turn the heap by lifting up the bin, placing it next to the pile of composting material, and then just turning the heap back into the bin with a fork. The small doors at the base of these bins are awkward for removing finished compost. I prefer to remove the lid and take small amounts from the top or to lift off the bin if I want to use all the compost in one go. My plastic bins produce lovely compost that's ready for use in 8 to 10 months.

Hot boxes

These tall, slim plastic bins seem like an attractive proposition in a small space, because they take up little room and the closed base means they can sit on a hard surface like a patio. They also have a tight-fitting lid, creating an enclosed system that is said to deter flies and rats, as well as reduce any odors. The insulated sides retain heat generated by decomposition with the aim of speeding up the process—some claim that finished compost can be produced in as little as 60 days, although I think most gardeners would struggle to achieve this.

Green and brown materials must be mixed in the correct proportions before they're added to the heap, because the aim is to produce compost without turning. Instead, material is continuously added at the top, while finished compost is removed from a door at the base. There is also a tray to collect liquid from the bottom of the heap and a tap to remove it. This "leachate" can be diluted and watered around plants, but I'm unconvinced that it is particularly nutritious. A hot box may be a useful option if you have a high proportion of food waste, but they are expensive.

Tumbler bins

These are designed to make turning compost easy, because the barrel-shaped bin is suspended in a metal frame, which you rotate using a handle. However, when I trialed them in my own garden, I found them to be ineffective, because any heat generated is lost to the air through the thin sides, meaning it can't hold heat to help speed up decomposition. Moreover, once the barrel is even partly full of material, it becomes heavy and it is more difficult to turn the handle. Coupled with the fact that they are expensive, I did not see any advantage in their design and would not recommend them.

Bokashi

A method of fermentation instead of composting, Bokashi is an alternative way to deal with food waste and might be attractive if you have problems with the smells from a kitchen caddy or are worried by rats in outdoor compost heaps.

It involves placing fruit and vegetable scraps, along with any meat and dairy waste, into a lidded Bokashi bucket with an innoculant containing effective microorganisms (EM). Anaerobic fermentation takes place, converting carbohydrates within the waste into lactic acid, in effect preserving the bin's contents and also producing a liquid that needs to be drained from the bucket via a tap.

In this fermented form, the food waste is readily digested by soil microbes, but the drawback is that it can't be spread on the soil surface. To fully decompose, it must either be added to a compost heap or be buried in a trench in garden soil, which would require additional space and cause damage to the soil ecosystem. I therefore only think it's worth the extra effort to reduce troublesome odors and/or if you have problems with pests being attracted to a compost heap.

WORMERIES

The decomposing abilities of small red worms (*Eisenia fetida*) (see pp.50–51) can be harnessed by keeping them in a dedicated wormery and harvesting their excretions (worm casts). This worm compost is ideal for mixing into propagation compost and produces excellent germination. A free-standing wormery can only process a small amount of waste and is possibly best for kitchen waste, in addition to a standard compost heap.

The right temperature range

Worms will not tolerate temperatures above about 80°F (26°C). This means you can't add too much green material in one go, because its decomposition would generate too much heat (see pp.43–44). Instead, feed worms little and often when they are active, which usually means at least once a week between spring and fall, when temperatures range from 54–80°F (12–26°C). In colder conditions, worms become dormant and do not feed, so to keep a wormery active during winter, you may need to move it indoors. Red worms will also be killed if they freeze, although their cocoons can survive.

Sourcing and feeding worms

If you have half-mature compost in the garden, it is likely to contain red worms, and that's all you need to populate a wormery. It's also possible to buy worms online, which works well. Worms feed on organic matter that's already partly decomposed, so they prefer finely chopped kitchen scraps that have already been

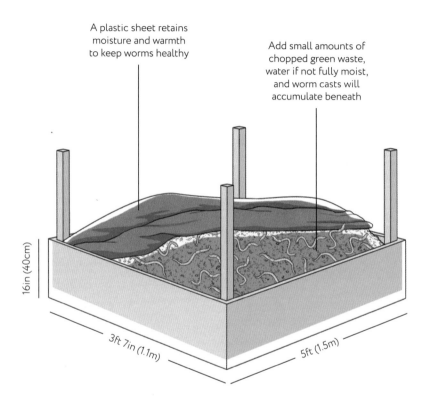

A plastic sheet retains
moisture and warmth
to keep worms healthy

Add small amounts of
chopped green waste,
water if not fully moist,
and worm casts will
accumulate beneath

16in (40cm)

3ft 7in (1.1m)

5ft (1.5m)

MY RAISED BED ENCLOSURE WORMERY

This simple design stands on soil and is
easy to construct with spare wooden planks
or boards and four short posts. Just add
worms and some chopped green material
to the base, cover with a sheet of plastic,
and you have a fully functioning wormery.

stored in a caddy for a day or two. Even better is half-decomposed compost, which is a treat for them if you have it. Worms won't work in dry conditions, so always add a sprinkling of water with waste and keep everything moist.

Choosing a wormery

Many designs of free-standing wormeries are available that can be placed on hard surfaces and are easy to move. However, these are vulnerable to temperature fluctuations and must be protected from freezing. Kits usually consist of a stand with stackable trays with holes for worms to move through and a close-fitting lid. Worms are placed in the bottom tray where they feed and breed, and a second tray is placed on top for them to move into once the first is full. Finished compost can be taken from the bottom tray after three to six months. Excess liquid from waste collects in a sump at the base, which has a tap for regular emptying. This liquid can be diluted and used as a feed for plants, although I'm not convinced it's rich in nutrients.

If you have space, a wormery that literally sits on the soil is what I would recommend, because it is much easier to maintain than free-standing designs. Try building a "raised bed enclosure," which is basically a box about 12–18in (30–45cm) deep; an open-based plastic box with a lid could work, but wood is better because it's more insulating. I started mine on weeds covered with wetted cardboard and placed worms and their food on that. A covering of black plastic retains moisture and planks of wood on top stop it from getting too hot when it's in full sun. Compost can be harvested after a few months by lifting off the surface layer containing the feeding worms and removing the deep deposit of worm casts underneath. Once this is done, the material containing the worms is placed back into the box.

OPTIONS FOR MEDIUM GARDENS

A busy medium-sized garden or allotment will produce a substantial quantity of compostable materials through the year, but even with this amount, be careful not to think too big. Always bear in mind that the most effective results will come when you fill a heap within two to three months.

Choosing suitable bays or bins

Bays with sides just over 3ft (1m) long (4ft/1.2m at the most) should be the right size for this volume of material, and make a simple setup with easy access for filling and emptying. I get fantastic-quality compost from bays constructed out of wooden pallets (see pp.114–117), which are easy and economical to build. Conical plastic bins can also work on this scale—seven large bins hold a volume roughly equivalent to two pallet bays—although you might prefer the appearance of bays, and they are cheaper.

Anyone with basic DIY skills could fashion their own bays out of bought or salvaged untreated wooden planks or plywood (see p.97). It's also easy, although much more expensive, to buy kits for constructing wooden or plastic bays. Wood is the material of choice, because plastic tends to bend and is not usually strong enough to make the sides of good-sized bays.

How many heaps?

Composting would be possible with one bay, but this makes turning its contents awkward. If you have enough materials to fill one pallet-sized bay within three months, then you will undoubtedly have enough to fill two or three. The ideal would be to have three bays in a line (see p.115) and turn the contents of the two outer bays into the middle one.

My routine is to fill one of the outer heaps in about two months, leave it for a month or two, then turn it into the middle bay. This is repeated in the bay at the other end, which can also be turned into the middle bay, on top of the older compost. The middle bay is then emptied about three months later, and it can contain as much as a ton of beautiful compost. Where there isn't space for three bays, two is workable, but finished compost needs to be used more quickly, as there is nowhere to keep it.

“ I get fantastic-quality compost from bays constructed out of wooden pallets, which are easy and economical to build. ”

CONSTRUCTING
A PALLET HEAP

Compost bays made from wooden pallets have a lot to recommend them. They are quick and cheap to assemble, the ideal size to receive all the material produced from a busy garden or allotment, and capable of producing a really useful quantity of wonderful sweet compost.

Materials and preparation

You will need four wooden pallets to build a single bay. It is important that they have not been treated with wood-preserving chemicals (see p.97), because these can be toxic and could contaminate your compost. Untreated or heat-treated pallets last between three and five years. I recommend removing the bottom section of each pallet, because it makes them lighter and less bulky and also makes it easier to access the contents of your heap. The only other materials required are strong, $^1/_8$in (3mm) thick wire and some sheets of brown cardboard, with any tape and staples removed.

Place the compost bay on soil (see p.96). Prepare the location by strimming or cutting down any tall weeds and leveling the soil if it is very uneven. A pallet bay can be built on top of lawn turf, rough grass, or perennial weeds, because these plants will not be able to grow through the thick layers of material added to the heap and will soon die off.

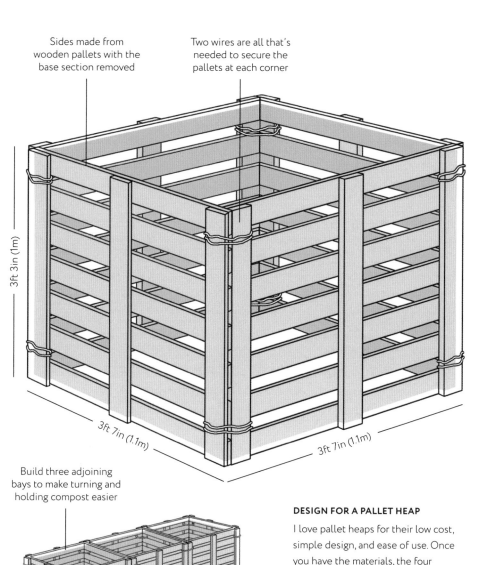

Sides made from wooden pallets with the base section removed

Two wires are all that's needed to secure the pallets at each corner

3ft 3in (1m)

3ft 7in (1.1m)

3ft 7in (1.1m)

Build three adjoining bays to make turning and holding compost easier

DESIGN FOR A PALLET HEAP

I love pallet heaps for their low cost, simple design, and ease of use. Once you have the materials, the four pallets can be quickly assembled and you can be filling your new compost heap in less than an hour.

Building your compost bay

It is not necessary to drive stakes into the ground to hold the pallets in place. All you need to do is lay out the four pallets on the ground so that they form a square at the base. Stand up two adjoining pallets with a right angle at their corner and secure their corners together by threading two lengths of wire through, one near the top and one near the bottom. Tighten each wire by twisting the ends together with your fingers or pliers.

Attach the third and then fourth pallet in the same way, thus forming a wooden box made from four pallets and eight pieces of wire. For easy access to the heap when turning (see pp.83–84) or emptying, just undo the two wires at one corner of any accessible pallet and swing it open.

Slot large pieces of cardboard under each pallet to cover the ground around the edges of the heap. These will block out light and help prevent any perennial weeds next to the heap from regrowing up and into the compost.

❝ For easy access to your heap, just undo the wires at one corner and swing the side open. **❞**

Tips for better results

A basic pallet heap is a great place to start, but a few simple additions will help improve the quality of your compost and increase the quantity that you can produce.

The sides of the compost bay don't need to be slatted to allow air flow into the heap (see p.98). Solid sides retain valuable moisture and heat, so I always line the inside of the pallets with thick, brown cardboard as I fill the bay, adding 12–18in (30–45cm) sections at a time.

Once the bay is filled, have a sheet of corrugated iron, black plastic, or something similar that you can cover composting material with to keep out the rain. This will prevent the heap from becoming soggy and anaerobic (see pp.54–55).

Only three pallets are needed to create each additional bay adjoining the first one. An empty bay next to the one you have just finished is a useful addition, because it gives you space to turn the compost into. Use three more pallets to build a third bay and you will have an efficient composting system.

My ideal setup has three bays: we put fresh materials in one of the side bays, then leave it to mature while filling the other side bay. No fresh material ever goes into the central bay, because that receives the turned contents from each side. First, turn the contents of the bay you filled originally, then turn the contents of the second bay on top of the ripening compost from the first bay. Leave this turned compost to decompose further for about two months to produce a full bay of compost that is ready to use.

OPTIONS FOR LARGER GARDENS

Along with a generous supply of compostable materials, extensive gardens provide the luxury of space to create a composting setup with several large bays to allow heaps to be turned. Be wary of gigantic bays, however, if you want the best-quality compost.

Avoid making bays too big

It's surprising how little the dimensions of the bays need to increase to provide a lot more compost. My large bays don't look much bigger than pallet bays, but they are about 2.5 times the volume—a big jump! If heaps are too large, they can become anaerobic in the middle (see pp.54–55) and take longer to fill, slowing the composting process down and making turning them a smelly undertaking. Check the volumes of different-sized bays in the Visual guide to sizes and volumes (see pp.100–103) to ensure that you build the smallest heaps to accommodate the available compostable materials.

I recommend building a line of sturdy wooden bays, similar to the row of seven bays central to my garden at Homeacres, which are a scaled-up version of the pallet bays (see pp.114–117). The simple design is straightforward to build and space efficient, and the adjoining bays make turning and emptying large quantities of materials and compost as quick and easy as possible.

The good number of heaps makes it possible to store compost as it continues to mature while also filling, turning, and maturing other heaps, which is ideal if you want to generate enough compost to mulch a large garden. I fill each bay within four to six weeks from spring to fall, and in about four months during winter. Then the contents are left to break down for a further one or two months before they are turned into a neighboring bay. Another advantage of my setup is that it has a permanent roof. This protects finished compost from heavy rainfall, which can cause it to become waterlogged, anaerobic, and smelly if a bay is left uncovered.

More heat, but less air

The compost from these larger bays is slightly darker than what is produced from pallet bays, even though the materials added are very similar, because these big heaps get hotter during decomposition and retain that heat for longer (see pp.43), promoting bacterial decomposition and reducing fungal activity. This has the advantage of helping kill more weed seeds (see pp.44), but the darker color signals the presence of fewer of the fungi that are a beneficial addition to the microbial life of your soil (see pp.19–21, p.24). Compost from large bays is still a wonderful mulch, but I particularly value the fungi-rich, lighter brown product from my slightly cooler pallet heaps.

The center of a large heap becomes a bit compressed under the weight of all the materials added, leaving little space for air and often creating anaerobic conditions (see pp.54–55). Turning the heap is particularly valuable for getting air into that middle portion, which aids aerobic and even decomposition. It is also a good workout and a fascinating chance to see how decomposition has been progressing.

CONSTRUCTING A BAY SYSTEM

I produce the bulk of my compost in seven large bays, built with a roof to keep out the rain. This sturdy structure needs much more time and skill to build than a simple pallet heap and has a long lifespan, so it is worth sourcing good-quality materials.

Designing and building bays

You could build any number of bays to suit the amount of material you have available. Three is the minimum number that would be worthwhile–if you can't fill three, then smaller pallet-sized bays would be a better option (see pp.114–117). I have seven bays that yield up to 9.9 tons (9 metric tons) of compost each year.

Each bay is 6ft (1.8m) wide and 5ft 7in (1.7m) deep, with a base that is open to the soil and a vertical 6 x 6in (15 x 15cm) wooden post at each corner. The full height of the posts used at the front of the bays is 8ft (2.4m), while those at the back are 7ft (2.1m) tall. But, because they are set in 12in (30cm) of buried concrete to stabilize the structure during windy weather, the steel roof slopes from a height of 7ft (2.1m) to 6ft (1.8m).

Within this framework, the solid wooden sides (see opposite) of each individual bay are screwed onto the corner posts. This makes them simple to unscrew and remove to provide easy access for turning (see pp.83–84) and emptying the contents.

Choosing materials that will last

I employed a builder to erect my compost bays in 2016, and his work plus the materials cost £3,000 (about $3,700). My aim was to create a structure that would last as long as possible. The vertical posts and roof timbers are softwood that was pressure treated with preservative to prevent rotting and prolong their lifespan. I would not generally recommend using treated timber to build compost bays to avoid any risk of preservative chemicals contaminating the compost, but these parts of the structure have little contact with the decomposing materials.

Initially, I used plywood sheets as a quick and convenient material to create the solid sides for each bay. However, I found these broke up in as little as three years and the glues used to manufacture some types of plywood may be toxic (see pp.97), so it's important to check the contents of any that you plan to use. Now, I use planks of Douglas fir or larch, because their high oil content acts as a natural preservative. Such wood is neither widely available nor cheap, but will last for many years without chemical treatment. See if you can source local timber with similar qualities.

Using a bay system efficiently

Every heap is turned just once, and when filling a heap, it is important to ensure a neighboring bay will be empty to receive the large volume of materials when turning. To achieve this, the first bay we fill is number two in the row, which is turned into number one. Then the second bay to be filled is number three, which is turned into number two after its contents have been turned into number one, and so on. By the time bay number seven is filled, the compost from the first two bays will have been used and we start the sequence again. If ever the compost hasn't been used in time, it can be emptied from the bays needed for filling or turning and stacked in other bays or a covered heap until it's required.

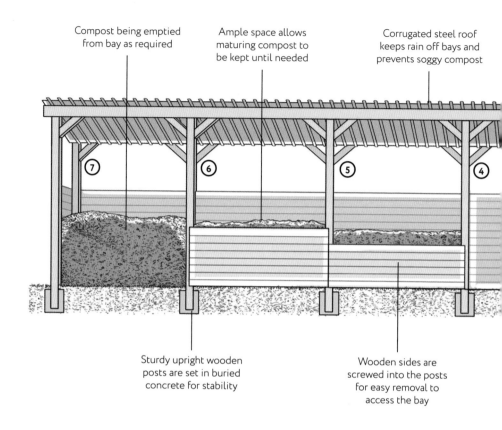

Compost being emptied
from bay as required

Ample space allows
maturing compost to
be kept until needed

Corrugated steel roof
keeps rain off bays and
prevents soggy compost

⑦　⑥　⑤　④

Sturdy upright wooden
posts are set in buried
concrete for stability

Wooden sides are
screwed into the posts
for easy removal to
access the bay

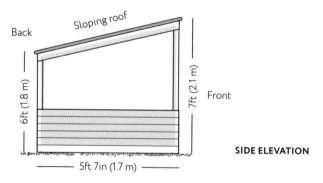

Back

Sloping roof

6ft (1.8 m)

7ft (2.1 m)

Front

5ft 7in (1.7 m)

SIDE ELEVATION

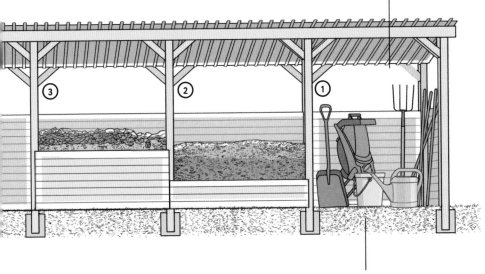

An empty bay provides storage for bean poles, pea sticks, and tools

Bays are built on soil to allow good drainage and access for soil organisms

SEVEN-BAY SYSTEM AT HOMEACRES

This stands at the heart of my garden and allows me to compost large volumes of materials and store the resulting compost until it's required. Investment in this kind of permanent structure is only worthwhile in large gardens. It is a pleasure to use.

1. Tools stored, waiting for turned compost
2. Maturing compost to be turned into bay 1
3. Current heap after 4 weeks of filling
4. Empty bay awaiting new materials
5. Compost, usually over 6 months old
6. Compost, 1–2 months younger than bay 5
7. Stockpiled 10–12-month-old compost, currently being used

SETUPS FOR BROWN MATERIALS

Carbon-rich, woody brown materials are broken down by fungi instead of bacteria and decompose slowly. Small amounts can be added to a regular compost heap, but large quantities of fallen leaves or wood chips are best composted in separate piles located on soil.

Wood chips

I value decomposed wood chips as a brown material to add to compost heaps and as a path mulch. Compost rich in wood adds fungal life to soil and feeds the soil food web, helping plants access nutrients (see pp.19–21). Where there is space, wood chips can simply be left in an open pile on the soil. Chips need plenty of moisture to decompose, but their structure stops a heap from getting soggy and means there's no need for turning. Only build a bay if space is limited or to reduce perennial weed growth.

The time it takes for chips to decompose depends on their size, freshness, and the type of wood. Large old hardwood chips can take 10 years to fully decompose, while small pieces of green wood will compost within 18 months.

Leaf mold

Fallen tree leaves may not appear woody, but are a brown material that's slowly decomposed by fungi over about two years. Make a dedicated pile for leaves only if more fall than can be added to your compost heaps in the following year. Don't build a bay—just make a pile of moist leaves, possibly covered with polyethylene to retain moisture. Large plastic bags with drainage holes can also be filled with moist leaves and left undisturbed to decompose.

USEFUL TOOLS
AND EQUIPMENT

Composting requires only a basic set of tools to chop or shred any woody or fibrous materials, turn or aerate the heap, and possibly check its temperature. These items help make composting faster and contribute to a more consistent result.

Pocket knife

Tough, thick herbaceous stems need cutting up before being added to the heap. A sharp folding pocket knife is convenient to carry in the garden and makes it quick to chop material as and when you clear it. Cutting is easiest if you slice stems diagonally, preferably when green. Regular additions of fresh material aid decomposition and avoid a build-up of materials to be cut later.

Pruning shears

An alternative to a pocket knife, pruning shears are less convenient to carry but ideal for cutting long or thick herbaceous stems. They can also be used to chop tougher woody prunings, up to about ½in (1cm) in diameter, into pieces no more than 4in (10cm) long for composting.

Hedge trimmer

A pair of shears is a great way of cutting hedges and pruning, but if you have larger hedges or shrubs, I recommend using electric hedge trimmers, because they are such an easy and quick way to gather material. They save so much time and are pleasantly quiet compared to those with gas engines!

Shredder

In medium or larger gardens, an electric shredder can really change the game, because it enables you to process and compost more woody material. Shredders crush stems as well as cutting them, increasing the surface area for fungi and bacteria to access and speeding up decomposition. My machine takes stems with a maximum diameter of $1\frac{3}{4}$in (4.5cm), which deals with the bulk of my woody waste. It does not work with green stems.

Rotary lawnmower

Long and fibrous bean, pea, and herbaceous stems; soft hedge trimmings; and fallen leaves can be chopped using a rotary lawnmower to help them break down faster and give an even and easy-to-use compost. Lay material on the ground, go over the top of it with the lawnmower, and collect the chopped material in the mower's box.

Shredder

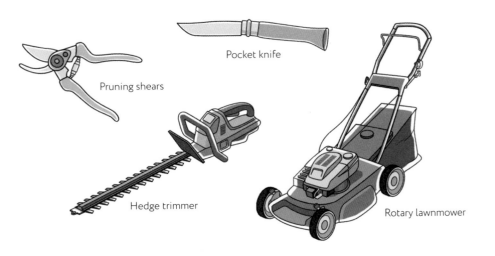

Pocket knife

Pruning shears

Hedge trimmer

Rotary lawnmower

Throw-through sieve

I do not advocate sifting compost before spreading it on the soil—there is really nothing wrong with a slightly lumpy finished product—but I do pass partially decomposed wood chips through a throw-through sieve before adding it to my compost heap. This piece of equipment consists of a metal frame with wire mesh of ¹⁄₂in (12mm) holes, set up on an angle of 45 degrees on its supporting metal bracket. When material is dropped from the top of the frame, the fine portion for composting passes through the mesh and large pieces fall down the outside. These are then collected and go back on the wood chip pile.

Compost thermometer

A thermometer with a long metal probe and a dial to read the temperature gives an instant indication of the amount of bacterial activity in a heap. Use this temperature reading to find out if and when decomposition is underway in a new heap, whether there is enough heat to kill weed seeds, or whether a filled heap has mostly cooled down and is ready to turn.

Manure fork

A manure fork has four narrow, pointed, and curved prongs that make it much easier to slide in and out of compost than an ordinary garden fork. It is also lighter, meaning you need less effort to turn, knock out lumps, and load compost.

Plastic shovel

Usually marketed for builders, plastic shovels are light and save a lot of energy when shifting bulky compost. They find the interface between compost and soil very easily, which makes them ideal for emptying the bottom of a heap and for shoveling piles of wood chips.

Aerator tool

This is useful where there isn't space to turn compost into a second heap, but it is hard work to use. Avoid designs with two hinged prongs, as these tend to break. Far better are those made out of a single piece of strong iron shaped into a corkscrew at the base. These screw down into a heap by rotation and are then pulled upward to bring lower levels to the surface and add air to aid decomposition.

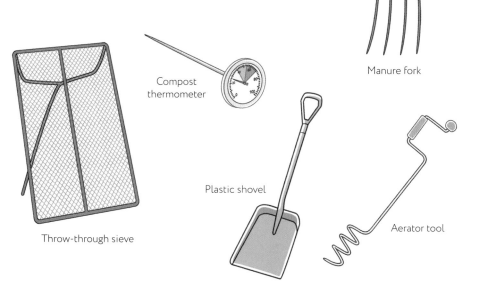

Manure fork

Compost thermometer

Plastic shovel

Aerator tool

Throw-through sieve

TROUBLESHOOTING

Gardeners come to me with all kinds of questions and concerns about their compost heaps. I'm happy to say that many are nothing to worry about and, with the right action, most problems can quickly be resolved.

My heap is a magnet for flies.

Fruit flies or fungus gnats around compost may be annoying, but they actually help early-stage decomposition. After that, their food source is gone and they will disappear.

How do I deal with smelly, anaerobic compost?

Wet heaps lack air and create sticky, smelly compost (see pp.54–55). Add air to your heap either by turning the materials with a manure fork to break open and aerate the lumps or by using an aerator tool (see p.129). Within a few weeks, the contents will be sweet again. If the wet compost is more than half decomposed, it can be spread on a bed, where it will quickly lose its smell and finish decomposing in the presence of air.

Is an ant nest a problem?

Ants contribute to the life in a heap and don't cause a problem when compost is spread. They will nest in dry, warm pockets of almost-decomposed material, especially where it has become quite fine. Reduce ant nests by ensuring material is moist and emptying a heap before it is too mature (see pp.85–86).

Why can't I make decent compost?

Everyone will have different expectations, but your compost is probably better than you think it is. Most homemade compost contains lumps and undecomposed bits. That's no problem, because you don't need perfectly fine, uniform compost for mulching (see pp.85–86). The important thing is to use the compost that you have and learn as you go along.

I have mostly soft, green materials to compost.

Green materials (see pp.64–65) contain a lot of moisture and don't have enough structure to hold air in the heap. This can quickly result in smelly anaerobic decomposition (see pp.54–55), but they make great compost when you add enough brown materials. During fall and winter, stockpile plenty of woody garden waste, cardboard, and tree leaves to mix with green materials during spring and summer.

My compost is full of weed seeds. What can I do?

Don't see this as a barrier to using your compost—just be prepared! When you see lots of tiny seedlings, tickle the compost surface with a hoe, rake, or trowel on a sunny morning, and by the afternoon they will have shriveled up. This remedial action is called a "weed strike." Once done, you can sow carrots, say, two to three weeks after spreading compost with weed seeds. Subsequently, fewer weeds germinate and are manageable.

How do I know when and how much to water a dry heap?

Any material that is crackling dry or dusty will not break down, because moisture must be present for decomposition to take place (see pp.42–43). Cut fibrous stems and woody materials into short lengths (see p.76) to avoid dry, air-filled gaps within the heap, and moisten dry materials using a fine rose or spray to keep water from draining through the heap.

Why isn't there heat in my heap?

Heat comes from the activity of billions of bacteria as they feed on nitrogen-rich green materials within a heap (see pp.43–44). Where there are few fresh green materials, in a small heap, during winter, or in dedicated heaps for wood chips or leaf mold, there will be little or no heat. You can still make fine compost–it just takes longer (see pp.56–57).

Will a compost heap attract rats?

Rats are always on the lookout for food and, in winter, somewhere warm to live; a compost heap can check both boxes. Rats sometimes arrive in my heaps in late fall and disappear in spring, which I can live with. If you're worried about rats, then remove potential food sources by not composting kitchen wastes.

Is herbicide contamination a concern?

If you make compost with materials from your garden, then herbicide contamination is unlikely. However, herbicides containing pyralids, which are sometimes sprayed on grazing grass for farm animals or used by gardeners in lawn weedkillers, don't break down during composting. If affected animal manure or grass mowings are added to a compost heap, then the contaminated compost can damage garden plants when spread (see p.34). Avoid contamination by checking that the growing practices of any farmers or neighbors from whom you plan to source materials do not involve the use of herbicides containing pyralids (see pp.34–35).

Why can't I make a bin full of compost?

Materials break down and reduce in volume as they decompose (see p.43), so even if you fill a heap over a long period, it won't be much more than half full by the time you use it. One cheat is to turn the contents of two heaps into one (see p.117), which produces a satisfyingly full bin.

There is white fungal growth in my compost.

White threads of fungal mycelium in a compost heap or sack are a great sign that fungi are decomposing woody materials (see p.45). Some silklike filaments may also be helpful bacteria called Actinomycetes that break down tough plant wastes.

How do I make enough compost to mulch my garden?

Add plenty of materials from outside your garden (see pp.78–79)— such as wood chips, farm animal manure, and garden waste from others nearby—to boost your compost production. Be careful to check sources for any herbicide use (see opposite).

Another alternative is to use less compost by applying a thinner annual mulch of, say, $1/2$in (1cm), which is still effective and allows a larger area to be covered.

INDEX

RESOURCES

CHARLES DOWDING ONLINE AND ON SOCIAL MEDIA

Website charlesdowding.co.uk

YouTube channel Charles Dowding

Instagram charles_dowding

Facebook CharlesDowdingNoDigGardening

TikTok charles_dowding

FURTHER READING

The Humanure Handbook: A guide to composting human manure by Joseph C. Jenkins (Jenkins Publishing, US, 2006)

The Compost Coach: Make compost, build soil and grow a regenerative garden—wherever you live! by Kate Flood (Murdoch Books, 2023)

Common sense compost making by the quick return method by Maye E. Bruce (Faber & Faber, 1973. QR Composting Solutions 2009)

Mycelium Running: How mushrooms can help save the world by Paul Stamets (Ten Speed Press, 2005)

Teaming with Microbes: The organic gardener's guide to the soil food web by Jeff Lowenfels and Wayne Lewis (Timber Press, 2010)

No Dig: Nurture your soil to grow better veg with less effort by Charles Dowding (DK, 2022)

Charles Dowding's Skills for Growing by Charles Dowding (No Dig Gardening, 2022)

No-Dig Children's Gardening Book: Easy and fun family gardening by Charles Dowding (Welbeck Children's Books, 2023)

Organic Gardening: The natural no-dig way by Charles Dowding (3rd edition Green Books, 2018. 4th edition Bloomsbury, 2026)

Dr. Elaine's Soil Food Web School [website], Dr. Elaine Ingham, www.soilfoodweb.com

REFERENCES

12–13 "Humus does not exist—says new study," Robert Pavlis, Garden Myths [web article], gardenmyths.com/humus-does-not-exist-says-new-study/

16–18 "Study linking beneficial bacteria to mental health makes top 10 list for brain research," CU Boulder Today, University of Colorado Boulder [web article], 5 Jan 2017, https://www.colorado.edu/today/2017/01/05/study-linking-beneficial-bacteria-mental-health-makes-top-10-list-brain-research

"Getting dirty may lift your mood," Christopher Lowry, University of Bristol [web article], 14 June 2007, https://www.bristol.ac.uk/news/2007/11797584419.html

22–23 White J. F., Kingsley K. L., Verma S. K., Kowalski K. P., "Rhizophagy Cycle: An Oxidative Process in Plants for Nutrient Extraction from Symbiotic Microbes," *Microorganisms*, 2018 Sep 17;6(3):95

24 *Entangled Life: How fungi make our worlds, change our minds, and shape our futures*, Merlin Sheldrake (Vintage, 2021)

25–26 "Fertilisers reduce plant-beneficial bacteria around roots," Rothamsted Research [web article], https://www.rothamsted.ac.uk /news/fertilisers-reduce-plant-beneficial-bacteria-found-around-roots

"Kicking the habit: fertilisers," Rothamsted Research [web article], 23 Sept 2022, https://www.rothamsted.ac.uk/article/kicking-habit-fertilisers

28 Eddie Bailey, Microscope images of soil aggregation (x400), October 2021, https://www.rhizophyllia.co.uk/about/

31–33 Cheng, Liang, DiTommaso, Antonio, and Kao-Kniffin, Jenny, "Opportunities for Microbiome Suppression of Weeds Using Regenerative Agricultural Technologies," *Frontiers in Soil Science 2* (2022), https://www.frontiersin.org/articles/10.3389/fsoil.2022.838595

Rinaudo, V., Bàrberi, P., Giovannetti, M. et al, "Mycorrhizal fungi suppress aggressive agricultural weeds," *Plant Soil* 333, 7–20 (2010), https://doi.org/10.1007/s11104-009-0202-z

TESTIMONIALS

Thomas Engel, USA

In 2021, I started copying your multibin compost I've seen in your videos. We wound up with almost a cubic yard of compost our first time through a season. This year, we're on the verge of at least 2 cubic yards of compost. This spring, I was able to spread about an inch of compost over 75 percent of our beds. We planted several types of tomatoes, peppers, herbs, and flowers in the improved soil. The outcome has been nothing short of spectacular.

June Williams, Wales, UK

After following your advice about composting, I got my heap up to 60°C [140°F] for the first time!!!

Beata Wypych, Poland

My new no dig flower garden is doing great in comparison to my neighbor's gardens. We have had a very hot June this year here again, but there was no such thing as a drought in my new garden at all. Everybody around's been complaining about drought but me!

Monja Smith, USA

Thank you for encouraging me (and so many others) to make my own compost, to bring in outside materials like bunny manure, leaves, and wood chips. I am now able to make really good compost in large enough amounts to cover my beds. My garden has improved tremendously with this method, I save money, and I thoroughly enjoy making compost.

Clive's Conundrum Garden, Canada

Thank you!! We finished our first batch a couple weeks ago. We trialed it against "Premium" bagged compost and Premium compost from a local facility. We were floored by the results. Turns out we can grow amazing produce. Glad we tracked and recorded it to prove it to our family and friends. We're expanding our compost area and will have it as our main priority as opposed to our last!!

Richard Loader, Dorset, UK

Since visiting Charles Dowding's garden and seeing his composting system, we have started to see our compost heaps very differently. Previously, weeding, trimming, [and] mowing seemed like chores, but now these activities have become harvests of food for what we now call "The beast." We gather the "browns and greens" and blend them so as to satisfy the appetite of the beast and enjoy monitoring the process of decay and heating with a long probe thermometer. It's like having a new pet!

Russell "The Free Radicals," Queensland, Australia

Even through the most challenging lack of rain and disturbed weather patterns here in South East Queensland where I live, no dig gardens have continued to produce, whereas most other gardeners in the area have given up on their production.

AUTHOR'S ACKNOWLEDGMENTS

My thanks to the garden team at Homeacres, notably Adam Wood for such great help in making, turning, and spreading compost. Also to Eddie Bailey for sharing insights from his microscope and to my son, Edward Dowding, for his photography and videography. I'm grateful to Chris Young for the idea behind this book and to Jo Whittingham for amazing help in writing and editing. I should also acknowledge the influence of Maye E. Bruce's book *Common-sense Compost Making by the Quick Return Method.* I don't use all her methods, but she is the first writer I've seen recommend a roof over heaps to keep rain out. What grabs me about her writing is the common sense part—always keeping composting simple and making it understandable.

PUBLISHER'S ACKNOWLEDGMENTS

The publisher would like to thank Vanessa Bird for indexing and Kathy Steer for proofreading.

Editorial Manager Ruth O'Rourke
Senior Editor Alastair Laing
US Senior Editor Kayla Dugger
US Executive Editor Lori Cates Hand
Senior Designer Barbara Zuniga
Production Editor David Almond
Production Controller Stephanie McConnell
Jacket Co-ordinator Emily Cannings
Art Director Maxine Pedliham
Publishing Director Katie Cowan

Editorial Jo Whittingham
Design Geoff Borin
Woodcuts Jonathan Gibbs
Line artworks Peter Bull Art Studio
Consultant Gardening Publisher Chris Young

First American Edition, 2024
Published in the United States by DK Publishing,
a division of Penguin Random House LLC
1745 Broadway, 20th Floor, New York, NY 10019

A catalog record for this book
is available from the Library of Congress.
ISBN 978-0-5938-4425-0

Printed and bound in China

www.dk.com

CHARLES DOWDING

Charles is a trailblazer in the field of no dig gardening and uses these methods to run his thriving market garden at Homeacres in Somerset, UK. He started his first organic, no dig garden in 1982, on 1.5 acres at his family's farm, having developed an interest in the link between soil and nutrition while studying at Cambridge University. This venture expanded and, by 1986, Charles was successfully cropping 7.5 acres and had begun giving talks and writing about his organic growing methods.

Homeacres is Charles's fourth garden, where he continues to observe and reap the benefits of adding a surface mulch of compost each year to feed life within the soil and boost plant growth. While his simple techniques have always grown healthy vegetables and fewer weeds, Charles has developed his understanding of the processes involved, and his teaching skills, too. He has never been afraid to question conventional gardening practices where there is no evidence that they are beneficial, and this "myth-busting" approach has helped him develop methods that improve results while saving gardeners time and effort.

Since launching the Charles Dowding YouTube channel in 2013, he has become aware of the amazing potential of new media to share and explain great ideas, information, and the beauty of his work with a worldwide audience. He creates diverse video content to inspire and inform anyone interested in no dig and composting. He also continues to produce numerous printed books, of which this is the first to look in depth at compost making.

Charles also welcomes visitors to Homeacres to take part in his no dig and composting courses, where they discover the benefits of using compost on the soil surface, which is radically different from the traditional approach of digging compost into cultivated soil. He is always struck by how participants' eyes light up when they see the compost heaps and is convinced that the composting process can provide us all with a meaningful connection to the natural cycle of life, as well as productive and beautiful gardens.